Freedom Revealed

Story of Onesimus As Seen in the Book of Philemon

Joyce Knight

"*I* hope you can help us locate the home of Philemon. We have traveled for thousands of miles to find him and have been assured that he lives close by. Would you be so kind as to direct us to where that might be?" the question was asked by definite newcomers to the area since everyone around was certain to know the exact house where Philemon lived.

Jerome, who had lived in Colossae his entire life knew that these men had never been here and he was rather hesitant in providing any unnecessary information. Their dress and accents distinguished them as coming from the west but he could not determine the exact location. "I might be able to do that, but I would first need to know the nature of your inquiry. I take it you are visiting or possibly just passing through, but for the protection of this outstanding man of the community, I would like to know you mean him no harm."

"We are just returning something that belongs to him and was taken from him many years ago." The men did not want to give away too much information.

"I am trying to determine where you call home. I cannot detect your accent and I am interested to know where you are from. I have not seen that particular design in clothing in the market around here, and I sometimes travel as far as Smyrna to do my shopping and do not recall seeing that kind of apparel being sold. I am just interested to know what your business with Philemon is." Jerome was determined to be as protective of Philemon as he could.

"We believe that what we have will bring him great pleasure in knowing that what once was lost is now found," one of the men answered, but that was only puzzling to Jerome.

"I do not see anything that you have that could possibly be of interest to Philemon. What could you have that would give him such pleasure, a man already of such means?" Jerome was feeling somewhat defensive for the sake of his good friend.

"You will only have to trust us that what we have will make him very happy. We are on a mission and as we said, we have traveled thousands of miles, taking us weeks to get here, to return to Philemon something we think he will consider of great value. We mean him no harm and only want to seek his pleasure. Please, we beg of you, trust us on this," one of the men answered in such a sincere fashion that Jerome could not but help trust them. Therefore, he directed them in the direction of Philemon's home.

Jerome could not remember Philemon having ever lost anything of great value, and he had been friends with him for many years. However, for some unknown reason, Jerome began thinking of an incident that happened to Philemon a great many years ago. Why now would such an event come to his mind?

Acknowledgements

As a first-time author, I would love to thank all those who stood by me and encouraged me along the way. Community Bible Study was my inspiration for it was there that the Holy Spirit gave me the nudge to even begin focusing on this topic. I appreciate my husband, Cecil, for standing behind me and not begrudging the time I spent in doing the research. I also wish to give credit to Jill who willingly shadowed this writing and inspired me to go forward. I hope that in reading this book, fiction none-theless, that you will appreciate the lives of such people as Onesimus and empathize with the life they endured.

Chapter 1

*I*f you wanted to find the home of Philemon, all you had to do was ask just about anyone in the community and he would have directed you to where ~~the~~ most powerful man in the area lived.

If you were coming from Laodicea, he would have said, "Go through town and turn right by the silversmith's building and down the road on the right, just a bit out of town. You cannot miss the expanse of land that is distinguished above all others that belongs to him. He is a very nice man and would love to have the company." Or if you were coming from the mountainous area from the north, you might be told, "Just go through the town of Colossae past the stone mason sign and keep on going until you come to a lovely home on the right and you will be welcomed by a very generous, fine man–a pillar of the community". Or perhaps you might have come from the south and you could have been given instructions from someone who would have told you, "Turn left onto a beautiful piece of property that has a magnificent home right in the center of it and you will be greeted by a very kind man and his family. But he was not always kind; he was arrogant and quite hard to get along with. But not now, no sir, a very kind man he is. Although he is no doubt the wealthiest man in the area, he has become quite benevolent. He greets everyone he meets with a smile and a sense of joy shows on his countenance. There are still some people who tend to shy away from him just because of how they remember he used to be. But now most men of the community agree that he has softened a lot, and he is quite eager to help out when there is a need, either financially or physically."

It was a beautiful spring day in the town of Colossae, but Onesimus was feeling very trapped and did not enjoy the kind of freedom the birds who were chirping and flying from tree to tree were experiencing. Also, he was thinking that the horses in the field did not know what being restrained involved. Today Onesimus did not feel free at all. In fact, on this particular day he truly felt tied down with no options for himself or any hope for the future. Why did he have to be born to a life of confinement and always be told what to do? Why could he not enjoy the life that was given to him?

His eyes just gazed upon the son of the man who delivers the fine materials used in the making of window coverings. He usually accompanies his father when they bring these beautiful colored fabrics to town. Why do they put so much emphasis on making their windows so beautiful when the one little cutout they call a window in the building I share with several people does not even have so much as a piece of sack-cloth on it. This Isaac does not realize how good he has it. He does not even appreciate the freedom he has to be able to come and go as easily as he does. He knew that Isaac was close to his own age and it made Onesimus feel very resentful to see how Isaac could enjoy life while he had no life of his own.

How wonderful to be able to walk up and down the road, go into town where all the activity was and enjoy talking and joking with other young men his age. That would be the life. "But what do I have in this place where I am only in submission to others? I have to always be here so I can be ordered around and not enjoy life at all." Onesimus was feeling very sorry for himself and especially resentful of his current situation.

His mother's voice interrupted his thoughts, "Onesimus, go get a bucket of water from the well so I can begin the noon meal." She knew he did not mind helping her out when he was available.

"Yes, Mother, I will be right there," but this time he spoke grudgingly. He realized that his mother worked very hard and he was usually anxious to help her out. He knew that whatever he could do for her was that much effort she did not have to put into her own labors. He strove to be available for his mother who was one of the women who prepared the food in the big kitchen.

It was a full day's work for the ladies in the kitchen to rub down the grain and prepare daily breads, fresh spices, special fruit dishes and process the meat; these were just a few of their tasks that occurred day in and day out. Even to heat water over the open fire and keep the dishes clean was a chore in itself. So for Onesimus to be able to collect the water for her took a weight off of her already overextended duties.

Onesimus took the bucket from his mother and could not help but notice the wrinkles in her hands. He knew that she had never been pampered or had the opportunity to have special skin treatments like the ladies from the big house. She deserved much better, and he frequently promised himself that he would one day make it up to her.

"If my mother and father had any idea of how I felt, they would be so disappointed in me. My parents and their parents before them have been under the control of this same family for as long as anyone can remember. They are nice enough as masters, but still I wonder what it would be like to be on my own and not be subject to the orders and threats that I have to listen to daily. I have not spent more than a few hours away from this property in my entire life. I hear that there are much worse masters to work for. Just down the road there are people who beat their slaves all the time for little reason and some of the taskmasters can be quite cruel. One man just the other day was beaten very severely for sleeping later than he should have and then taken and thrown down a cliff to die. I believe we are purposely allowed to hear such things to make a point and to be used as an example of what could actually happen to us. I hate to think that my "people" would be like that, and I really think they are much kinder than most owners." These thoughts often went through Onesimus's head, but he knew he could not share these thoughts with anyone else; and it would not do any good even if he could.

"Here, Mother, is your water; what else may I do to help you out?" As he set the bucket down beside her, he noticed that his mother had a large bruise on her forearm. He did not want to bring attention to it for fear she would not want to explain, and he knew she did not want him to worry. "Onesimus, you are so kind to ask, but do you not have chores of your own you are supposed to be getting done? You surely have not cleaned out the stables yet, and you know how they like having them done by noon," his mother said with anguish in her eyes. Her behavior was quite unusual, but had been becoming more of a pattern.

"I am on my way, but Mother, you just look so very tired this morning. Are you feeling all right?" Onesimus often worried about his mother because of the hard work she did. She was on her feet from sun up to sun down and never had anything to look forward to from day to day.

"It's just that I miss being with your father, you know? Since they started the new rule that all the men must sleep in one building and the women in the other, it has been very difficult for both of us. I really do not get to see him much anymore and it bothers me that Barnichle, who took charge as headmaster over the servants, decided separating the men and women would be more productive. I hate it that he has been put in the position to have authority over us and be able to dictate whatever we do." Leithia, Onesimus's mother, said this as she continued to knead out the bread in preparation for a big dinner that was being planned for some of the church attendees in the community. Since Philemon's home had become host to the local church meetings, there had been more activity and catering of many elaborate meals.

"There just has to be a better way of life. There just has to be," Onesimus thought as he headed toward the stables. "Where and when will I be able to do what I want and when I want?" It had been his parents' lot their entire lives to be under the control of others; would it be his also?

He had to come up with a plan, and he had to be sure it would work. One way or another, he had to do something to make life worth living.

As Onesimus looked across the yard, he noticed that a group of men had just gathered in the big house as they did periodically. "I wonder what they do when they get together. They seem like very refined men of the community, but on occasion I notice that some of the more common people also come. So there is a mixture of all kinds of men from around the area that meet here with Philemon. Maybe I can just take a peek in the window on the side of the house there." Onesimus's curiosity got the best of him and he found himself climbing up on some pieces of stone that had been placed alongside the wall close to the window. He only hoped that he was quiet enough not to be noticed because he knew if someone spotted him eavesdropping, he would be in a great deal of trouble.

"This seems to be a very strange meeting for leaders of the community. They are not talking about people who I know and they are not discussing governmental issues or Roman rule at all. When distinguished men and leaders of the community get together, I would think those would be the topics." Onesimus was definitely at a loss as to the purpose of this meeting.

"I will love Thee oh Lord my strength. The Lord is my rock and my fortress and my deliverer; my God, my strength, in whom I will trust, my buckler and the horn of my salvation and my high tower. I will call upon the Lord who is worthy to be praised; so shall I be saved from mine enemies." Onesimus distinctly heard this being read from some sort of tablet. He momentarily grasped the concept of what was being read and lingered awhile since it was beginning to interest him to some extent.

"He delivered me from my strong enemy, and from them which hated me; for they were too strong for me." He went on to hear words that sounded very lovely. "The Lord liveth and blessed be my rock, and let the God of my salvation be exalted." He thought he heard something about a Psalm and wondered what that was? This all sounded very good , but Onesimus had trouble believing that grown, strong, robust men of the community took time out to just sit around and listen to someone read to them. The only time he had seen that happen was when the nursemaid read from a parchment to Master Philemon's little nephews when they came out and sat under the fig trees. Deep down Onesimus knew he was feeling very jealous of the luxury they enjoyed, and he desired to be able to read like that.

Onesimus did feel somewhat prideful as the esteemed men treated Philemon, his own master, with such admiration. He could tell that they all certainly trusted and had complete confidence in everything he said. He was definitely an authority figure and that made Onesimus proud.

But witnessing this made Onesimus want to strive even more to accomplish great things and be able to have the opportunity to be somebody someday. He knew that unless he did something about it, he would always be a nobody . "I guess I should just be happy for what these other people have — at least that is what Mother always tells me."

Sometimes getting up to face a day full of sunshine makes everything better again, but not today. Onesimus is still thinking things through as he enters the kitchen.

"Onesimus, dear, you appear especially troubled today. I noticed yesterday you seemed a little down, but it's more obvious today. What is it? What can I do to help you?" Onesimus's mother, even through her own pain, acknowledged something was amiss with him.

Onesimus set down the bucket of water he had just drawn from the well in the back yard and realized he had not hidden his feelings very well.

"Mother, will it always be like this? Will I forever have to be at the mercy of others? Will my life never be my own? I cannot help but think that it should not be this way. I see people my age come and go as they visit, arrive for parties, wear their fancy clothes, make deliveries, and they usually seem so happy. They live their lives for themselves, never realizing how it would be to have to account for every move they make and never make any decisions for themselves. I wish I could just one day be like that Isaac." There! He had finally expressed himself to someone.

"Oh, the ambitions of youth. I remember when I was your age, I felt the same way. However, I know times are different now and you desire your independence. Young people today are just so impatient. But, Onesimus, do not wish too hard for things that will never happen. You will just be more disappointed and you must realize that this is your lot in life. There is nothing your father and I can do about it since we were born into a family who are owned by others and that is just the way it is." Leithia knew her words were falling on deaf ears.

"Oh, Mother, I cannot imagine you and father ever wanting to leave here as bad as I do. You just seem to be so compliant and content." Onesimus knew that she just did not understand.

"We have really done the best we could do and tried to make something good out of the situation we are in." she sadly said.

"I just cannot imagine being here for the rest of my life." Onesimus realized he did not want to hurt his Mother and realized he should just drop the subject.

"Maybe one of these days there will be a revolt of all the slaves in the Roman Empire and we will be free. But do not anticipate that happening in our lifetime," Leithia added in order to leave Onesimus with something to hold on to.

"Could that possibly happen? Might it be that we could oppose all the powers over us and overthrow them to give us our freedom?" Onesimus found delight in the thought of ever being made free. His mother had just given him new food for thought, and that is all it took to encourage him to put his plans into motion.

"I understand that the slaves in the Roman kingdom far outnumber the dignitaries and overseers and from what I hear, there are 60,000,000 slaves in the whole Roman Empire. I overheard someone who came for Master Philemon's church meeting not too long ago say that if the slaves only knew how many millions of them there were, owners could be in serious trouble. But you know, Onesimus, that we have no access to weapons or any way of defending ourselves." Leithia looked a little sad as she shared this with her son.

Onesimus suddenly got excited "You mean there are a lot more of us than there are of them? How exciting to know that."

"But you must realize that in so many cases, we do not know who all the other slaves are. They do not make it easy for us to join ranks. As you are aware, all of the workers here dress alike, but when you go out in public, you are not sure who you are actually meeting. We have our clothes made from the same bolts of material to distinguish us from workers from other homes and institutions. You may not realize it, but a lot of the masters in our area and especially from big industries do not clothe their slaves in the same type of garments or colors. They do that so they will not be recognized as slaves." Leithia realized that she too wished it could happen.

"You mean that if I would ever be able to go to the village, no one would know I am a slave? People may not recognize me for who I really am?" Onesimus was excited at the thought.

"Well, let us not get too carried away. There are still ways that a person can be identified as a slave. Look at how poorly made your garments are and look at your sandals. Did you ever see people going in and out of Master Philemon's house who actually dress as poorly as we do?" Leithia wanted to bring Onesimus back to reality.

Onesimus began thinking about something his mother had just said. "What do you mean "clothe" their slaves so they might not be recognized? I realize that we all pretty much wear the same thing here and definitely I know who to take orders from and as you said, our clothing is poorer quality from those who are not slaves, but please explain what you mean."

"Well you see, some masters believe there could be a revolt if the slaves got together. Think about the fact that when they run errands in town and meet each other on the streets, there could be conversations between servants that would get things stirred up. They make sure that some of their servants wear shades of browns, others blues or dark yellow, some multi-colored such as stripes or color blends, and some garments are knee length, others longer. The fabric and the styles are all different and try to blend in with 'regular' people so slaves in the community do not stand out and are not uncommon to a certain group. This would lessen the opportunity for gatherings and revolts to take place. You would not know a slave from a master in some instances so there would be less opportunity for an uprising. Even though the quality in appearance is different, sometimes you just do not pay that much attention if you are not dressed exactly alike." After she thought about all the issues, Leithia was less certain that getting away from that lifestyle would ever happen.

"Regardless, someone needs to take charge and build forces and get all the slaves together, unite and get an army together of us all to pull ranks–that would show them. And where would they be then without our free labor?" Onesimus boldly said to his mother.

"Do not say that and please do not let anyone hear you talk like that. You can plot this in your own mind, but you are just a dreamer." She was saddened that her fate had been passed on to her precious Onesimus. "Please know, dear, that they will never allow that to happen. For one thing we would not be able to leave our residence here to connect up with others nor could they unite with us. If there were a place where a large number of slaves work for a big establishment, you can be sure they are well guarded to prevent any kind of dissension to take place."

After feeling somewhat disappointed in what his mother had just said, an excitement came over him and with a glimpse of mischievousness, he said "Mother, you can be sure I will not be here the rest of my life. I am looking forward to a better life and intend to see to it that it happens."

"Shhhhh, Onesimus, please do not speak of this again. This could never happen. If our masters even suspected you were thinking of any kind of conspiracy, it could be the death of all of us. I have heard stories of men who have tried running away, but they were usually always caught." Leithia's heart raced at the thought of losing him.

Onesimus now looked discouraged as he asked, "What happened to those who did try to run away, Mother?"

Appearing to not want to speak of it, but knowing that Onesimus needed to be certain of the consequences, Leithia shared what she knew with him. "Your cousin Andre' tried to escape about six years ago, and he was caught about three miles away–off the road in a low-lying area. They brought him back and with a hot iron, branded him with the letter "F" on his forehead so that everyone that saw him was reminded that he was a 'fugitive'. Then after a while he was taken to Philemon's relative, which is quite a distance from here and we have not seen him since. But he is a living reminder to everyone there that trying to escape does not pay. And he does not have nearly as good a life there as he had here. Please just appreciate the fact that you are here under the control of Philemon. He is really a good, kind man. We could have it a lot worse. I must add that Philemon's character has changed over the last few years. He seems much softer. The other slaves and I often discuss the transformation that has taken place in his life within the last few years. Whatever happened has been a definite advantage for us all."

Onesimus left his mother's presence knowing in his heart that he had to devise a way to get out of there. He did not want to get his family in trouble so he had to come up with a plan that would work and keep it to himself. Regardless of how nice a person Philemon was, he could not give Onesimus the true freedom he dreamed of.

Chapter 2

As the sun rose early in the eastern skies, so did Onesimus. As usual, he was up before most of the others in his quarters and began the normal duties that he was expected to accomplish each day. He had the responsibility of caring for the animals and keeping the stables spotless clean for his compulsive taskmaster. He consistently came in to check his work and there better not be anything out of place or insects to be found in the feed. It was a good thing that Onesimus was also meticulous so there had not been a problem between the two of them. Actually, Onesimus went above and beyond the call of duty. Not only did he keep the animals bedded down when not in use, but he also found out that he enjoyed building step stools and little carts that were helpful in the barn area. Frequently, he had been commended by the men who came to use the donkeys and horses on how helpful the stools had been in when mounting the horses. They also realized how convenient the carts were in taking things to market and returning with a load. On occasion Onesimus would be complimented by Roual for his fine carpentry. He never let it interfere with his main job of maintaining the barn or caring for the animals. He just found that he enjoyed using his talent of working with wood and told himself that it was therapeutic. Today was going to be much different than all the rest; Onesimus had determined that this was the day. He had to appear as though it was like any other day and not arouse suspicion to anything out of the ordinary. He hoped that he could act normal and not be too anxious about what he had in mind. He was confident that his plan would work and he had to hold on to that thought.

After a hard day's work and when everyone appeared to be settled in for the night, Onesimus quietly got up from his tiny bed where he had given the appearance of being settled for the night, and went to the quarters where his mother was staying. He gently knocked on the window that was close to her bed and tried to get her attention without arousing any of the other women in the room. Amazingly, she acknowledged him and went to the door where they met.

He gave her a hug and very tenderly said to her, "I know that you have tried your hardest to be the best mother I could have possibly asked for all these years and you have done your best to make things as smooth for me as possible. I realize that you have worked very hard and I know your health has been faltering lately, so please try to understand in your heart that I love you and will always be thinking of you. Please let Father know that I cherish him and honor the fact that he has been so very loyal to Philemon. I admire his perseverance in responsibilities that he has taken on here and that the two of you have dealt the best you could with the fate that was given you. This is not how I can have it be for me, though, so no matter what happens, please know that I will always love you and whatever the outcome, this is something I have to do for myself and it will be worth the risk. If my plan does not work out, then it will not have been in vain for I could never be happy in this life."

Leithia noticed a new type of maturity in her son that she had never seen before. She wondered what had gotten into him and this new drive was really scaring her.

"Onesimus, what are you saying? No, if it is what I think, you cannot do this. Please do not take any chances. You know I could not live thinking something terrible had happened to you." His mother realized no matter what she did or said, she would not be able to stop him. She was startled at his new attitude as he looked so determined in whatever he was planning to do.

With tears in his eyes at the thought that he may never see his mother again, the only person in his life who he had ever felt any connection to, he gave her a hug and turned away.

He had to somehow say good-bye without her truly knowing what he was planning so that when questions were asked, she would not have any information to give.

His mother looked around the room and it appeared that no one in there heard a word, and if they did, it was in everyone's best interest to keep quiet. Her fear at that point was that information would get out and a greater risk would be awaiting her precious Onesimus. She lay back on her meager cot and silently cried. "Onesimus, what are you doing? What are your plans? Could I have tried harder to change your mind?"

As he left her quarters, Onesimus quietly headed to his bunk and noticed that all the others who shared his quarters appeared to be sound asleep. He realized that he too should be totally exhausted after the strenuous day's work he had put in. However, amazingly enough, he had a phenomenal burst of energy. After picking up a few supplies, he tiptoed out into the darkness as his heart sank wishing he could take others with him so they too may share in the freedom he was so looking forward to. He realized that his heart was beating so hard and fast that anyone within a few feet could surely hear.

As he approached the front gate, he quickly passed a cart that had appeared to be abandoned, and he noticed a pouch that apparently had been left by Philemon's officer. He remembered hearing about the sale of some leather goods and this was no doubt from that transaction. Could he? Should he? Before he realized what he was doing, Onesimus's hand reached for it and tucked the bag under his tunic; he hoped that it would contain something useful he could later use. Off he went down the lonely dark road with his heart skipping every other beat. He was suddenly startled when he heard a noise off to his right and knew for sure he had been caught. As he slowly turned around, he realized it was a small animal of some kind that had knocked over a jar on the edge of a table that was several feet behind him. Onesimus breathed a sigh of relief, but knew his course had just begun and there would be potential for a lot of close calls ahead.

He did not think anyone would be up and around at that time, but just to be sure, he headed through the field and was careful to avoid the main roadway. On occasion some of Philemon's family members would sit out in the cool of the evening and talk for a while, but he thought that it was a little late for that tonight. Sometimes there are Roman authorities that roam the countryside and he definitely did not want to be caught in the act by any of them. He thought he would need to come up with a story if someone captured him. "I know, maybe a colt had run away. Yes, that is it, I am running after a colt."

The whole entire world to him now was dark, very black, and very creepy. Every little sound he heard was magnified in his mind. "What have I done? I can hear my heart beating so hard and loud that it feels as though it is going to explode," Onesimus thought to himself as he continued to run, run, run down the field, and hoped that he did not run into any wild animals that he could not handle. He had remembered to pick up a knife on the way out, but knew it would be much too small for anything very big and he would have to be so close to make it useful. He had never had this kind of feeling before, which was mixed with fear, anxiety, and loneliness, but mainly release. In all his illusions of being 'trapped' and how desperately he wanted to be free, he still had never felt unsafe. He knew he had always been protected and sheltered. There had never been a fear of wild animals venturing into the yard because there was always too much activity and even if they had, there would have been too much protection from the guards who walked around. He had never had to fear vicious men or bandits before–until now.

"What if I end up running in circles? What good will this venture be to me? How am I going to know if I have been here before? Everything appears to look the same. I did not realize it would be so flat and open here. He kept wrestling in his mind that everywhere he turned, it looked the same. I feel so desperate now. Let me think about some of the stories I have heard the men talk about who have come back from trips. I need to just settle down, yes calm down, stop and analyze a plan. Of course, I remember now to keep my eyes on the stars or the moon, and continue to look up. 'The stars are all so different', the old men said and 'to follow a certain one because it will be the guide.' So Onesimus looked up and sure enough there was one star in particular that was quite a bit larger, more radiant than the others. He would keep his eye on it for direction. Onesimus realized that helped a lot and gave him assurance that he was doing something correct. At least by concentrating on the sky for direction, he was able to divert his attention to something positive.

Onesimus had to take a breath from his running. He thought that the faster he ran, the further the distance would be between himself and the house from which he had come. He knew he was in good physical condition, but he also understood that he still needed to pace himself. He began to just walk along for a good while but then it was time to begin a heftier pace and he resumed to once again run for a bit. As he was moving at a pretty brisk pace, something caught his ankle and down he went flat on his face. His heart began to race and knew it was all over. He was ready to turn himself in because he knew he had been caught. But how did they sneak up on him so quietly that he did not hear or realize they were so close? So many things passed through his mind in the few seconds it took for him to slowly turn to see who it was that had him when he realized that a tree root had nudged its way out of the ground and had caught itself around his ankle. What a relief for Onesimus as he untangled himself and took time to wipe away the perspiration from his forehead. He was having a hard time believing he was actually saved from what could have been a fatal encounter.

This had become the longest night of his whole life and he was thinking that he could have been lying comfortably in his own little bed, safe away from the creepy noises of the dark fields, the horrible encounter of running for his life, and the fear of the great unknown. He knew if he could just get through the night, he would have made the right decision. But it was still a few hours until daylight. Would he make it? Would he even be less safe then?

The next morning, Caleb went to the stables to see where the mule was that usually awaited him at the post. He had looked around and realized something was amiss. When he discovered his mule was still bedded down, Caleb knew something was wrong. At once he began the inevitable scurrying around to try to locate Onesimus. Everyone knew that Onesimus took pride in having the mules readied for their day's duties. It had been this way ever since he had assumed this position 18 months ago. There had never been a day that Onesimus had let them down.

Caleb at once went to the building where Onesimus slept, but to his dismay, no one seemed to have missed Onesimus since he had always been up way before the others on a daily basis. "I want every one of you to spread out and find him. Bring him to me. He had better have a good explanation as to why he has shirked his duties," an angry Caleb shouted.

The report came back to Caleb that there was no sign of Onesimus anywhere. All the other slaves began to tremble with fear that something terrible had happened to him. They had not a clue as to where he could be.

"Onesimus has family members around here, does he not? I believe his mother works in the kitchen. You, lead me to her," Caleb demanded of one of the older servants.

As Caleb, who was escorted by two of the grounds' guards, entered the kitchen, Leithia's heart sank as she dropped the jar of meal she had just opened.

"Which one of you is Leithia, the mother of Onesimus?" Caleb shouted out, bringing fear to all the women in the kitchen.

All eyes shifted toward Leithia as she responded, "It is I, sir. What can I help you with?" She tried to compose herself and act as if this would be her first inkling of Onesimus's decision.

"Where is your son, Onesimus? He did not perform his duties this morning and is nowhere to be found. If you know what's good for you, I demand you tell me immediately where he is." "I… I am sorry, but I do not know anything. Is he missing? I did not know but what he would be where he was supposed to be. Please believe me." Leithia began crying realizing Onesimus had carried through with whatever he had been planning.

"You appear to know something; otherwise why did you drop your container of meal? See the mess is still before you. What do you know?" Caleb believed something was amiss.

"I will clean up my mess, you can be assured, but sir, you did startle me when you charged into the room. I do not know where Onesimus could be. You must believe me." Leithia spoke so assuredly that Caleb could not help but think she was telling the truth.

"I will take you at your word, but if I find out that you have lied to me, you will wish you were never born." Caleb stormed out of the room into the courtyard gathering up all the men he could to help in the pursuit of Onesimus.

"No, I have not seen him and have no idea what could have happened to him" Onesimus's very worried mother said to another officer who came into the kitchen. Her worst fears apparently had come true. She had to be sure and conceal her anxiety in order not to give away her fear. Onesimus apparently had decided to look for that better life he had so often talked about. "I do not know where he could be. Have you looked really well in the area where all the animals are kept or maybe he is getting a supply of food for them?" She thought at this point that she should come up with anything that might stall for time. At least she would be able to give Onesimus a chance to get as far away from here as possible; after all, he was on foot and they would begin looking for him on horseback.

"Of course we have looked everywhere that he could possibly be, woman. Do you take us for idiots? He is nowhere. He is gone. Tell me what you know about his whereabouts. I know you have a close relationship because I see you together quite a lot. He must have told you something. Out with it. You are not helping yourself by holding back." A very angry officer drilled Leithia quite harshly.

Tearfully, Leithia replied, "Please, please do not take this out on me. I do not have any idea where he is. This is news to me. I am worried sick about this. Master Caleb came by earlier inquiring and that was the first news I had of his leaving. If you find out anything, would you please inform me so that I may be at ease?"

"Since it is obvious that you know nothing, let us not waste any more time here. However, if we find out that you know anything at all and are holding it from us, we will be back and you will be so sorry," one of the brutish men said with anger in his eyes. "We will continue our search before we have to approach Philemon with the news." The men left very upset knowing this news could mean trouble for them personally.

Sobbing, Leithia spoke softly to herself, "Onesimus, what have you done? Where are you? I pray to the gods that you are protected. Please, please keep him safe." Leithia had never felt so frightened in all her life.

"Are you sure you have looked everywhere? I cannot believe that bag of money has just disappeared. Think, think, think — where did you leave it Simeon? That was a goodly price I received from selling that leather and I cannot have it misplaced." Philemon questioned the officers about his missing pouch after it was disclosed to him that it could not be accounted for.

"I have thought it through very carefully and know it was safely put away." But Simeon had realized that he had accidentally left it on the cart and if Philemon knew that he messed up, he would be in deep trouble, so he had to come up with something fast.

The conversation about the money bag was abruptly interrupted by two men rushing into the room. "Master, master, we just got word that one of our young slaves has disappeared. We have looked all over the perimeter of the land and he is nowhere to be found." An anxious officer explained to

Philemon even though he realized he had just interrupted an already disturbing conversation.

"Please tell me who it is" Philemon demanded. He had not had a slave escape for many years and remembered how difficult that situation was to handle.

"It is Onesimus, the son of Erastus and Leithia whose family has been in your father's possession for generations. He is gone–nowhere to be found. We have checked with Leithia and Erastus, but they seem to know nothing. What should we do?" the officer asked.

Simeon realized he could be saved at this point and knew where to shift the blame for his own negligence. "Master Philemon, I would be very certain that this Onesimus has taken the pouch of money and run with it." Simeon thought to himself that Onesimus could be his scapegoat, and there was a chance he was actually the thief who took the money.

"Get teams of horses mounted and search the entire countryside. He could not have gone far. I trust that he is on foot and would need a time of rest. Search for him. Also did you check to be sure none of the animals are missing? I would hate to think that he rode away on one of our prize horses. Onesimus is one of the main people that looks after them. Is that correct? Please give me some answers." Philemon was upset but thought through all the angles that needed to be covered.

"Yes, sir, we have made a count of all the livestock. Every one of them is accounted for. He is definitely on foot. We can be certain of that." One of the men had been prepared for that question.

"Then go find him. Search everywhere. He must surely be close. He would not know his way around the countryside at all and it is reasonable that he has been traveling around in circles. You will surely find him not too far away. Bring him back to me and I will deal with him when he returns." A very angry Philemon knew now he not only needed to avenge a runaway slave but also a thief. He had never been able to tolerate someone who he could not trust.

Philemon realized that what he had said must have come across very harsh; consequently, he had let his human nature take control and not thought through how his Lord would have wanted him to react. He took a deep breath, whispered a little prayer and knew he had to retract some of his spoken words. "If you find this Onesimus, please be sure to do him no harm, but bring him to me and I will speak with him personally. I will counsel with him and find out what is going on," Philemon said in a calmer voice as he called out to the men as they were leaving.

The last time Philemon had to deal with this issue, he had not as yet become a Believer. He was excessively severe in dealing with the situation then but would approach it differently now.

Two of the men discussed among themselves how they had as yet never been on a hunt for a runaway. "This may be the most excitement we have ever had. What a day this may turn out to be for us."

"Yes, I agree", chimed in the other, "I hope we do find him. We deserve to finally have some fun."

Chapter 3

"I cannot believe how tired I am. I knew being up all night and tramping through the countryside would be exhaustive, but I did not prepare myself fully for how wiped out I would be. How thankful I am to be below all the mountainous area that is just to the north. Admittedly this path I have taken has been bad enough, but climbing up and down those hills would have made the trip much harder. Also, I understand that by not going that way, I have avoided notorious robbers that would just as soon kill me as look at me once they got what they wanted. Those hills would make a great place for people to hide and be able to jump out at passersby." Onesimus thought to himself as he trudged on. He could not help but think back to some of the stories that had been told as people had sought shelter at Master Philemon's house. He had overheard episodes of robbers who did not care who they hurt, just so they got a little fortune. He also knew about people who were filled with some kind of demon possession, who would jump out at anyone that came by and be as a mad animal and supposedly were not accountable for their actions Their homes were said to be in the caves, but I cannot imagine anyone actually living there. These were the things that brought fear to Onesimus. Things he tried desperately not to think about.

"The thought of all this demon possession and fear of thieves overtaking me did make the time pass by though." Onesimus actually found himself laughing to himself.

As he felt a hunger pain, he was so glad he had thought ahead to stash away a few provisions for his trip. He had been on the run all night and had not thought about eating or drinking, but now, the natural instincts are taking over. He sat under a tree and brought out a piece of bread and flask of water. "This will refresh me, or at least it has to do for a while." He knew he did not dare stash away too much or else he would have brought suspicion to himself. Since he did not have much in the way of food, he would hope to be able to use his money to buy something somewhere soon.

"The sun has now risen and I am sure that by now I will have been missed by someone." Onesimus began to tremble a little at the thought that people would be out looking for him. "If they catch me and take me back, it will all be over. I do not want to think about the consequences right now. I have to keep on moving and must trudge on regardless of how very tired I feel."

After going on for about two or so miles, Onesimus took time out in the open field to look around, enjoy the beautiful scenery and warm morning air. As he stood there with his hands rubbing his achy, tired back, he was in awe of the view. No one in sight, just he and the beautiful flowing countryside unique with amazing fields and mountainous terrain as a back drop. It was all so still, somber. As he gazed across the plains, he could see the hills in the distance with the sun making its way above them. Squinting his eyes, he could almost see some people grazing their sheep in the distance. That is something he had only heard about. Mostly, from what he had heard repeated his entire life about there being indignation toward shepherds. Onesimus could never understand why, except that they were considered lowly people. He could not understand how anyone could be lower than a slave like himself, his family and the others he associated with, but then there were the shepherds. Mainly, he recalled the Roman guards that came by belittling the common shepherds because they were dirty, uneducated, and just beneath any other type of people. He never understood why taking care of sheep was so demeaning because to Onesimus, it looked like a perfect task to have. They get to be out on their own with no one to order them around and could do pretty much what they please. "What was so bad about that?" Onesimus thought to himself.

As Onesimus began to move on forward he suddenly had a feeling of relief. "I have never been out in the open spaces like this before. As far as I can see there are fields and everything is so still and huge. I kind of like this a lot and wish I could live in this peace and tranquility all the days of my life, but I am afraid that would be living in a fantasy world. It is just a matter of time until there will be a search party looking for me I suspect". Any peace that Onesimus felt quickly changed to anxiety again at the thought of what could be coming his way.

"To think of all the times I listened to the old men talking about directions, looking up to the sky to point the way. I see now that the moon and stars are always in the same place and at the same time of day during certain seasons. I recall how travelers told of stories of getting lost, but remembered to look up for guidance. It seemed to work for me last night so I will look to the sun during the day because the sun always rises one direction and sets in the other. I am so glad at this point that I listened carefully not knowing how greatly it would benefit me". Onesimus pondered how he kept his eye on a certain bright star in the sky all night and followed it so that he would not lose his way.

"I will tread on a little further and maybe I can find an out-of -the -way spot or even a big rock where I would not be noticed. Oh do I feel I need to take a little rest if I am going to be able to go on", Onesimus took time to look around to see if there was an isolated place. "Look, a culvert under that bridge over there. It looks to be perfect to lie down for a while and rest my weary body." Onesimus took a few steps hoping when he got there he would find a safe spot and where he could find comfort and not too much water that would make him wet," After all these are the only clothes I have, but this does look to be an ideal spot to rest up a little before I continue on." Onesimus crawled into the hole and before long found himself getting very comfortable and drifted off to sleep.

Suddenly he was startled by the trampling of horses' hoofs that approached the bridge overhead. Onesimus could not believe he had been found. They were actually here. Should he give up easily, or go with them kicking and screaming? There must have been four or five riders that stopped on the bridge. "We have been looking for hours now and do not see the lad anywhere." One of them said as he realized they were dis-mounting. He could hear their feet hit the wooden floor of the bridge right over his head. They began pacing back and forth and the sound of their feet rattled in his ears. "He couldn't be that good to have gone any further than this. He probably went the other direction anyway. He's just a stupid slave boy and not worth our time. Let's go on back and tell Philemon that we scoured the entire countryside and he was no place to be found. If anything, a wild animal probably came along and devoured him." Onesimus heard one of them say and hoped that the others were in full agreement.

"I am sure that you are right. At night especially this area is notorious for foxes and there could have even been soldiers come from the west that found him and imprisoned him or worse. It is very obvious that he is a runaway and any Roman soldier would have jurisdiction to do with him as he pleased." The men were willing to give up and head back to Philemon and that was just fine with Onesimus.

"I can't believe that they could not hear my heart beating so hard within me. I thought it was going to jump right out of my chest. The thought of these men being right over me was terrifying. I am just glad they gave up so easily. As long as Philemon accepts the news that they could not find me, that is great with me. Maybe he will believe the part of my being eaten by wild animals and dismiss ever looking for me again." Onesimus talked himself into feeling more at ease.

"What am I saying? Wild animals could be lurking around here. What if they do attack me and eat me. I have never seen a fox before, but I understand they are very fast and can latch onto you with their sharp teeth. I remember hearing a story about someone long ago defeating wild animals with a sling shot and pebbles. I need to look around and see if I can find some kind of defense." Onesimus found a large stick and a couple of rocks in addition to his little knife he already had. Now he was much more encouraged by the extra protection he had acquired.

Chapter 4

"Ok, now the sun is to my back and since it is still morning that means that I am headed west. I need to keep assuring myself and pay attention to it moving up above me. I think that is what I remember from the old men while listening to their conversations. I need to keep heading the way I am going and all will be well. I do need to keep my eyes and ears open to be sure I am not spotted. I fear I am in the open and could be easily spotted. I do not know how often soldiers pass by in this part of the country. I am not very close to a road, so surely I will be safe from them." Onesimus kept talking to himself and hoping that what he was doing was the right thing.

"I wonder how long it will be before I come to a town or see anyone at all. Just look at me! How dirty and unappealing I must be if I did run across someone. There is no question but what my clothing is that of a slave and that my general appearance looks like a vagrant. When the time comes that I meet up with someone, I will definitely be viewed as a run-away slave. It sure would be nice if I could somehow have access to a change of clothes. But how could that ever happen?" Onesimus was almost too tired to really care.

The day was a hot one and traveling along the fields out in the open with nothing for shade was also something Onesimus had not thought through. He did not remember ever being this tired before, and he had to watch his water supply and stretch it out. The work he was used to involved being in the shelter of the barn with little time under the hot blazing sun. "I do not understand where the wonderful breeze is that blows at Philemon's property. I could always count on a pleasant soft wind even on the hottest of days. I suppose I have run into more of a desert condition and that makes the difference. Oh well, I must remember to accept the good along with the bad."

Just then Onesimus heard a rustle in the field very close to his feet. He froze and looked down to see a viper ready to attack. All he could do was stand very still thinking that any further movement could set it off. He decided to wait it out and hope for the best. He could feel the perspiration run down his back in fear of an attack. He vividly remembered the words that came from the house of Philemon on many occasions as the men in worship would call out, "Oh, Lord our help in time of trial." All Onesimus could think of was to repeat those words. He felt that if he ever needed help, it was surely now.

As suddenly as the viper came, it disappeared. Onesimus felt such a relief come over him. It was almost as if repeating those words "Oh, Lord our help" made all the difference. He must remember that.

As much as Onesimus enjoyed being an independent worker while he was a servant, and loved being left alone, he desperately would love to see someone at this point. The sun was in front of him now and it was the hottest part of the day. He was trying his best not to drink all his water just in case there was no change in his traveling pattern. He did not realize how lonely life could be without being with anyone for this length of time.

As Onesimus looked far in the distance, it appeared as though there was a little house ahead. "Surely I am seeing things," he thought. "There would certainly not be a lone house way out here in the middle of nowhere." As he ventured on in that direction he began to realize that it most certainly was a dwelling. "It is. Yes it is a house. I cannot believe there may be help in store for me after all." As excited as he was to see the house and to think of there being some kind of help for him, Onesimus was also apprehensive.

"What if the inhabitants do not take kindly to visitors? What if they are vicious and intend on harming me? Or what if they realize I am a runaway slave; would they try and sell me to someone who would be cruel to work for?" All kinds of negative feelings flowed through Onesimus's very being

"It is worth the risk. Since I no doubt have already been spotted anyway. I must go ahead and hope for the best. I am going to have to be in contact with people sooner or later, and it might as well be now." Onesimus talked himself into being brave as he pressed forward.

"Do I dare go there and check it out, or should I avoid it? What would Father do?" He pondered this as he was getting closer to the house. As he drew closer, he saw a lady coming out with a little child toddling along beside her.

Apparently she had not noticed him yet since she looked to be getting ready to draw water from the well that she was walking toward. Onesimus reluctantly walked toward her but was unsure as to what her reaction would be to a stranger's approach.

She looked quite startled at first, but when she realized he meant her no harm, she beckoned him to come closer. Although he noticed she looked a little skeptical, he reached his hand out as a gesture of peace and acceptance. She was still a little hesitant to allow her son contact with him until she understood why he was here.

"What are you doing way out here all by yourself? It is very unusual to find strangers just walking along." The lady held tight to her little one and trusted that all would go well with the young man coming toward her.

Onesimus knew he had to come up with a reason for being out here all alone and an excuse for being something other than a slave. Since she was fairly young and living so far removed from everyone else, maybe she would not recognize his clothing as anything other than normal.

"I do believe that I am lost. I have never been to this part of the country before and am not sure what's ahead of me. I could use some direction as to what town I am close to, or maybe I should rephrase that and instead ask, 'how far is the closest town to here'?" Onesimus needed to know how much farther he would have to walk to get to someplace, any place at all.

"Well to tell you the truth, the closest town of any significance at all is from the direction which you came. That would be Colossae. Also, not far from here is Laodicea. But you are headed away from both of those places." The young woman did not know if she was of any help to him since he looked a little disappointed.

"Then I guess I need to know information regarding the direction that I am headed. Do you know how far I would have to travel to find something that way?" Onesimus hoped she would say 'not very far' but based on her previous comment and her expression, he was prepared for the worst.

"A few day's journey by foot, for sure." She realized that is not what he wanted to hear but it was the honest answer. "If I remember correctly, it is about 100 miles to Ephesus which would be the closest town from here going in that direction."

"Are there others in the house? Are you and the boy alone here?" Onesimus hoped he was not going to be overrun with others who may suspect him of being a runaway.

After a little hesitance, the lady answered honestly. "The boy and I are the only ones here. My name is Tisha and my little boy is Julian. It has been several weeks since we have seen anyone pass by. Our home is not on the road, as you can tell, and that is the way my husband wanted it when he built the house here so we would not be prey to passersby. And that certainly worked out as very few people come this way. Those who do have been harmless enough, mainly thinking they are taking a shortcut or looking for property that has not been settled. Please come in. You really look as though you could use some refreshment. I do not have much, but what I have, I will gladly share with you."

Onesimus helped her with the bucket of water. Suddenly he realized he was no longer so tired, but felt a burst of energy as he carried the bucket into the house for her.

The lady watched Onesimus very carefully and trusted her instincts to believe he meant her no harm. "As I said, we do not see many people so it is a pleasure to have guests stop by. Tell

me, have you been traveling far? And I did not get your name."
Tisha was very curious as to the reason this young man was
way out here all alone with no particular destination.

As Tisha took out some bread from a sack cloth and a little
piece of meat that looked as though it was the last food in the
house, he wondered how she was surviving. How did this
young woman care for herself and the child apparently all
alone? She mentioned a husband, but where was he? Many
thoughts were going through Onesimus's head but he was
careful not to be too presumptuous. He did not want to do
anything that may cause her to be too defensive.

Onesimus was not quite sure how to explain the reason he
had come here. If he said he was from Colossae, would she
get news any time about a slave who had run away? He was
feeling so full of guilt at that moment that he was hesitant
about how the formalities should go. Somehow the words just
came out and he felt very comfortable with her and secure in
saying, "My name is Onesimus and am from Colossae, but I
am wanting to go to a bigger city and see what other parts of
the world have to offer." He hoped he would not have to go
into any more detail than that because he was not very good
at making up stories. He knew he had run away and stolen,
and he did not want to add lying to his list of sins.

"Onesimus," Tisha repeated, "Now that is certainly a name
that I have never heard. I understand that you may have

wanted to leave from wherever you came from, but why did you decide to come by yourself? It is very risky traveling these roads all alone. You appear to have just taken off on your own just to go somewhere or anywhere, is that right? Do you have a plan at all?" Tisha's curiosity got the best of her and she thought she would get her questions asked while he was ravenously devouring his food.

"Oh, no real plan. I just decided to take off and see what was out there. I have never left the house where I was born and wanted to venture out for a while. This is quite different terrain than what I am used to. But the trip here was very beautiful. I saw shepherds for the first time today. I have heard stories about them and now I know they really exist." Onesimus tried to think of something else that would divert the attention from him.

"The countryside is quite populated with shepherds. They sometimes come very near to here in hopes of finding better pasture for the sheep. I always enjoy having them graze close by. They usually come over and talk, give me some of their meat, and even lend me a hand here with my chores, and in return, I will bake cakes for them and allow them to wash up." Tisha noticed that he was interested in this other way of life and thought she could at least enlighten him to keep the conversation going. Tisha, herself, was deprived of adult companionship and this was a ray of sunshine for her to be able to have someone to talk to.

"You do not know how glad I am to have you here. This is like a very bright spot in my day for me to see people." Tisha was feeling quite confident in his being there.

Onesimus had not realized how hungry he was and how good it was to sit at a table and enjoy a meal with such pleasant company.

"I am sorry that I do not have more to offer you, but things have been pretty sparse lately for us. Our life did not work out as we had planned." As Tisha began to talk about her life, she appeared to look very sad as she wiped away a tear from her cheek.

"I do not want to pry because it appears you have had some difficulty, but where is the boy's father? What happened that you ended up here alone? I must admit that I am rather surprised to find someone such as yourself being here all alone. Do you mind sharing with me?" Onesimus knew she wanted to confide in him and thought if he prodded her a little that it may make things a little easier.

"My dear husband, Ebeneezer, passed away three weeks ago with the fever. It has been very difficult for me trying to be a mother and father to little Julian. I have tried to work the land and feed and water the animals but it is more than I can endure. I have held on as long as I possibly can." Tisha spoke with such sadness that Onesimus could hardly contain himself. "I just recently found someone to take the few animals I had and I am just going to leave my house and anything else I cannot take with me."

"So you are leaving and giving up what you have here?" It was hard for Onesimus, who never owned anything in his life, to understand how someone could abandon their possessions.

"After much thought, I have decided to pack up and move on. I am leaving tomorrow to be with my family in Miletus. I have been so saddened by Ebeneezer's death that I did not have the energy to get things together sooner. It has been a hard decision to also leave the home that we had built together, the dreams we had here. This is where we planned to raise our children. I now have made the decision to pack up what I can and go ahead with the move. I have some things ready to load on the donkey first thing in the morning and then head out. I will have to leave several things behind, but I just cannot handle any more. I certainly do dread the trip, but I have no choice." Onesimus had never been close to anyone who had lost a loved one and he really did not know what to say to comfort her.

"Whatever I can do for you, I will be happy to. If you are leaving tomorrow, then I will travel with you. If you would have me be your companion, that is." Onesimus, for the first time in a long time was not thinking of himself, but truly had Tisha's welfare in mind.

"I really was not looking forward to traveling by myself. Julian and I would have to travel so slowly and it would be a long, hard trip. I was remembering when Ebeneezer and I came, we were so excited to find this place that we did not mind the venture at all, but now it is totally different. I have been feeling so alone and fearful." Tisha's demeanor changed from gloom to partial brightness as she continued. "It is like a miracle that you are here. Yes, I would be overjoyed to have you accompany us. However, do you have a desire to go to Miletus? It is a seaport town, but has become somewhat unrestful due to strife between workers who wanted more of a democracy and that is one of the reasons Ebeneezer wanted to leave and start a new life. However, it is still where I call home and I need to be there now."

"Going there suits my purpose and I do understand the travel could be very dangerous, but I have had little trouble so far in my trip. However, I would feel very badly for a woman traveling by herself with a young boy to care for. It would be my pleasure to make the trip together, and I will go wherever you are planning since I do not have any plans of my own." Onesimus was dancing with joy inside but was refraining from showing too much excitement.

As Tisha began cleaning up the table from Onesimus' meager meal she looked a little down and stated, "I am a little disappointed that I was not able to provide for you more."

"Oh, where are my manners. Thank you so much for the delicious meal. I guess I was so hungry that I overlooked the part of being grateful for it. Please forgive me for not showing you how much I appreciate your hospitality." Onesimus was very disappointed in himself for not acknowledging her kindness sooner.

"Oh no, I did not mean that. What I meant was that I am embarrassed about not having more to offer you. It is amazing how little it takes for Julian and me and with the plans to leave, I did not have anything stored up. I have already put aside everything I have for the trip tomorrow to sustain us as we go. I knew you were appreciative by the way you were feasting on what little you did have." Tisha was quick to atone for his manners.

"If you will show me what you intend to take, I will be happy to get things loaded for you. The less you leave behind, the better you will feel about it." Onesimus knew he needed to be very helpful since he realized she was having a very difficult time with all of this.

"All I planned to take with me was provisions that would fit in the bags I will throw on the donkey's back. There is no question that I will walk all the way while leading the donkey with

Julian strapped on. I will only load on what can absolutely fit which will mainly be a few clothes, and a little food and water for us along the way," Tisha said with a definite sadness in her voice for the thought of leaving so much behind.

"We must go ahead and turn in to get a good night's rest since it will be a hard trip ahead. I am so tired; I know I will go right to sleep as soon as I lie down." Onesimus did not know what he would call a bed for the evening, but knew that the floor would do.

"You can take Julian's bed for the night. I know it is a little small for you, but it would be better than the hard floor. He will sleep with me. As tired as I am, though, I am so excited that I may not get very much sleep, so if he is restless, it will not matter much." Tisha prepared the bed for Onesimus and she then readied herself and Julian for the last night in her home.

"Thanks for your hospitality, and good night." Onesimus spoke feeling somewhat uncomfortable since this was the first time he had ever shared a room with anyone of the opposite gender.

"This is a very strange feeling that just came over me," the words came from Tisha's lips before she realized what she was saying.

"What is that? What do you have a strange feeling about?" Onesimus's curiosity was aroused.

"Every night since Ebeneezer passed away, I have been so frightened in the evenings. I am always so fearful that someone or something may break in. You never know who may pass this way and need to get in for shelter or with intentions of doing harm knowing that I live here alone. But tonight is the first time that I feel at ease. I feel so comfortable with you here. I do not know you, yet it is all right and very peaceful. I feel relaxed enough that I may actually get a better night's sleep than I have had for ever so long. Also I generally wake up each morning dreading what may happen to us during the day. So I am convinced that I am no worse off getting out of here and taking my chances on the road even as much as I dreaded making the decision to do that." As Tisha spoke she assured herself that all would work out well.

"I can understand your sense of fear because I know my trip so far has not been an easy one emotionally. My being a man and more able to run and hide if necessary is easier than for a woman with a child." Onesimus tried to reassure her that his being with them would be an added comfort.

"Excuse me for saying so, Onesimus, but you are hardly a man. I do feel a lot more secure with your being with us I admit, but a few more years would more likely classify you as a man." Tisha had not had the pleasure of laughter for quite some time and it felt so good.

"All right, I get the message." Onesimus replied and was so glad the darkness kept Tisha from seeing the embarrassment on his face. "But I am getting there and cannot wait."

Chapter 5

As the riders drew closer to Philemon's place with news that Onesimus was nowhere to be found they were fearful as to how Philemon would handle this information. They did not realize that Philemon had been in constant prayer over this situation and he had chosen God's direction for whatever the outcome, as well as of the control of his anger if it came to that.

"He is not going to like this and I hope that he will not take his anger out on us," one of the men who looked for Onesimus said to one of the others as they approached the front door of Philemon's house. "We will just have to assure him that Onesimus probably was attacked and carried off somewhere. He will not blame us then, you can be assured." He came back with the response that he thought would work.

To their amazement, Philemon was very reserved, "Master, most owners of runaways would be totally upset and seeking revenge. Are you thinking of a plan to get retaliation on his family members who also are workers here? What do you have in mind for them? We could help you with ideas according to what we know other slave owners have tried."

"Justus, Justus, do you not know by now that is not my style? As much as I feel deceived and my heart aches that I have been violated, you should realize that I have a standard to live by and that is of forgiveness. I would not avenge the mistakes of this boy onto his hard working father and mother. That is the old way, not mine. I have previously shared with you the experience I had when I met Paul of Tarsus while I was doing business in Ephesus and how he instructed me on the ways of the love of the Lord Jesus Christ. Since then I have not had that kind of hostility you speak of in my heart. Paul made me aware of love for my fellow man. Yes, I feel sad that Onesimus would ever leave here because I sensed a closeness somehow to his family even though I had no real personal contact with him. From a distance I had my eye on him and took note of what a dedicated worker he was. It has greatly disappointed me in knowing now that he has left without a word. I have established a lifestyle for the slaves that would make it as easy as possible for them to want to remain here, not only out of duty and a sense of ownership, but that this is their home as well. Especially since they do not live in harm's way from the outside world of which they know nothing. I wish I knew what got into him that would make him leave the most comfortable way of life a slave could possibly have." Philemon reinforced his values on these men as they looked at him in amazement.

"But Master, how about the bag of money that he took? Does that not provoke you to anger just a little? You were deceived and you do not care? Do you not want to make up for that in some way?" Simeon interjected as he had been listening close by and wanted to be sure Philemon was reminded where the blame should go in order to keep it away from him.

"Yes, that indeed bothers me, but I also blame the carelessness of the one who left it in open view. I know very well that you tried to cover up and I am well aware of your reprobate mind, Simeon." Philemon spoke most assuredly.

"We will not use Onesimus as a scapegoat. Let us just go about our duties of the day. Forget this happened and pray that the Lord is looking over Onesimus and keeping him safe. We will probably never see him again. God bless his soul." Philemon was troubled by the entire incident but rested in Christ Jesus' sovereignty to make the situation a blessing.

Philemon is now reminded of his many conversations with Paul when he was in Ephesus and Paul was on one of his many journeys. "I remember as if it were yesterday that while I was on a buying venture in Ephesus, I met up with Paul at the home of my dear friend, Gaius. He instructed me on The Way and the power of the Holy Ghost that is given to believers. I, along with other new converts, was baptized in the name of the Lord Jesus Christ. Those times spent in the company of Paul and the other believers were the best opportunities of my life." As he remembered Paul's words, he peacefully left to check on the new well.

"That man is amazing. I do not know how he can have that kind of attitude. Not me. No way. I would bring Erastus in and take this misfortune out on him for not keeping control of his own son." Justus spoke confidently as he watched Philemon head down the hill toward the well.

"Philemon, dear, what seems to be the problem? You look sadder than I have seen you for years. Is there something that I can do to help?" Apphia kept her eye on her husband as he walked toward her.

"Apphia, my beloved, I have some news about one of our young servants. It is Onesimus, the son of Erastus and Leithia. He took off in the night. I sent men out to look for him, but he was nowhere to be found. They have returned with news that he must have been captured or worse. I feel so very saddened that this has happened, but trust that the Lord is with him if, indeed he is still alive." Philemon confided to his wife of his sadness as they walked down the path to the new well.

"Oh, no, I find that hard to believe that one of our own would run away. Did he not realize how good he had it here? When he finds out what the world out there is like, he will be wishing he were here where he was safe and cared for. I did not have any real connection to him, but I am aware of Lethia. I believe Onesimus is one of the young ones, and we know how their minds can work, whether free or slave. What are you going to do about it?" Apphia inquired realizing how hard Philemon was taking the news of his runaway.

"I will do nothing but pray for his safety and trust he will be well. He made his choice, now he will have to live with it." Philemon informed Apphia of his decision to not dwell on harboring resentment.

"It bothers me, though, to see you taking this loss so hard. Is there anything any of us can do?" Apphia questioned.

"Let us get word to Archippus and Epaphras so that the elders of the church will have special prayer for this boy. It will soon be time for Epaphras to leave for Rome. After receiving word that Paul is needing him there, all Epaphras has thought about is to go visit with him and be of some encouragement. So I will call on support from him while I can get it before he leaves." Philemon decided to locate them and have prayer together.

Philemon found Archippus and Epaphras in earnest discussion over the saints of his charge. "I feel confident leaving this church body in your capable hands, Archippus. I know that while I am gone, you will be a solid, faithful leader and you are well equipped in the pastoring of the church. You will take this responsibility very seriously. I do not know how long I will be gone, but as long as Paul needs me, I will be there for him." Philemon found them speaking of their future plans for the local church after Epaphras's departure.

"What brings you here?" Archippus saw his father, Philemon at the door and noticed that he looked sad.

"It appears that one of our young slaves, Onesimus, son of Lethia and Erastus ran away in the night. And worse than that, he apparently stole a bag of money from the sale of the leather yesterday. I am saddened by his leaving and also about the loss of the money, but I am more concerned about his welfare. You know he has never so much as set foot outside the perimeter of our property. I just have my doubts that he will be able to survive out in a world he has never known before." Philemon noticed how startled they were at the news.

"I have sent for the other church leaders and they will soon join us for a time of prayer together at his home. We have needed to draw together anyway and continue to support you, Epaphrus, in your upcoming journey to join Paul in Rome." Philemon opened the Scriptures to Psalm 20 as they waited for the others to come.

"Greetings, brothers. It is always a pleasure to have you meet with us." Philemon, Epaphrus, and Archippus greeted the others with a big body hug.

"We are not clear on the message we received, but we are here to do whatever we can. If prayer is the key, then that is what we will definitely do," one of the men spoke knowing that was the best resource he could ever offer.

Philemon explained the situation and also could not stress enough how they needed to cover as well the trip that Epaphrus would be making to Rome to join Paul. The men knelt in Philemon's front room where the meetings were usually held when the leaders of the church got together.

After a time of prayer together, they arose, arm in arm with the strength of the united body which meant so much to each of them.

"Since I have received the Lord Jesus, I am striving to walk with Him. I work hard at putting my past life behind me and live as the Lord Jesus would have me. Before I met Paul and listened to his teachings, I would have been quick to avenge my loss of Onesimus." Philemon was actually full of joy as the men left his presence in knowing that he was doing the right thing in moving on and he would continue to pray that Onesimus was protected from harm's way and that the peace of the Lord Jesus would be with him.

Tisha slept better than she had since losing Ebeneezer. However, she thought she was still dreaming when she heard a clanging just outside her window. On scurrying to see what it could be, she noticed Onesimus hard at work with tools and pieces of wood.

"What in the world are you doing so early in the morning? The sun is barely up and you are doing what?" Tisha was quite stunned to see a little cart on the ground as Onesimus turned around to acknowledge her.

"I did not mean to arouse you, but I kept thinking during the night of a way we could take more of your things with us and I decided to get up and see what I could find. I was very thankful for a full, bright moon and I remembered where you left the candle, so I got started on locating some wood and thought I could put together a little cart to help carry whatever you did not want to leave behind. You know this donkey is strong enough to pull a lot of weight and I think what I have designed will work out just fine." Onesimus stood back and looked at what he had made with great pride.

"I had no idea you had the ability of a carpenter. This is great. I am so excited to be able to take the little table Ebeneezer made for me as well as the silver cups given us on our wedding day, and oh, yes the kettles he got for me before coming here. I can take all of our clothing and the bed linen and..." There was no end to Tish's excitement.

"I hate to let you down, but there is a limit as to what this wagon can carry and what this little donkey can pull. You might just want to start loading things that are the most important to you and we will hope for the best." Onesimus was very glad that what he had done was so pleasing to Tisha.

"Onesimus, before we get started, I really feel that you do need to have a change of clothes. I believe you are almost the size of my late husband and I just happen to have some of his things right here. Take them and I will show you the best place to wash up. You will feel much better about yourself once you get those things off and a new change of clothes on your back." Tisha could sense the excitement in Onesimus's face as he accepted the garments. She also was wondering what his situation was. She believed she knew what the type of clothes he was wearing represented but she could not say for sure. She would dismiss any negative thoughts from her mind and only trust their time together would be well spent.

"I am really grateful for these clothes. They will work just fine. I do remember resting under a bridge the other night and I suppose that did no good to my clothes. This is great and makes me feel much better." If Tisha only knew HOW much better the new clothes made Onesimus feel. At least now he would not be spotted as a runaway slave.

It was amazing how much of what Tisha wanted to take actually fit into the wagon that Onesimus had made. As he looked back at the little dwelling before departing, all that was left behind was the bed and couch and two or three odds and ends that could easily be replaced. "Whoever comes across this house will always wonder why it was built here in the middle of nowhere and why it was also vacated." Onesimus thought to himself as Tisha said her goodbyes to a life that once was.

"I cannot believe how quickly the three of us got up, loaded the little wagon and the donkey and were on our way even taking time to eat the little breakfast that I had put aside. I pray that the rest of the trip goes just as smoothly. I need to concentrate on looking ahead, not back and keep telling myself that I have made the right decision to move on," Tisha said as she trudged along.

"Yes, you were quite ambitious this morning, I must say. And little Julian seems to know good things are ahead since he was very cooperative as well. I do not think you had a choice in the matter other than to leave and start a new life." Onesimus realized that Tisha still needed encouragement about having done the best thing for her and her son.

"I believe it is going to be a very hot day. I am so glad I had vessels of clay with lids to keep enough water cool for us to last awhile." Tisha thought out loud, Then she continued with a mixture of sadness as well as anticipation in her voice, "You know it has been three years since I previously made the journey coming from the other direction. Things were so different then. Ebeneezer and I were very excited. We did not have little Julian to travel with us, and I did not mind the trip at all. This is very different, indeed."

"It appears that life does change. You can plan for a long time and when it finally happens, the reality of it all is hard to believe. It is not easy deciding if a right decision has been made. I suppose we will find out soon, won't we?" Of course Onesimus was speaking for himself but Tisha had no way of knowing that.

"You sound very astute for such a young person. It is almost as though you have traveled down this road yourself." Tisha felt assured that her traveling companion could read her thoughts.

"Please forgive me for being so forward. But you, too, look very young to have already been left a widow and to have a small son. You have had a very sad young life. Can you tell me more of your life and a little of what brought you to this point in your life?" Onesimus thought this was a very good time to get to know Tisha as they traveled along.

"I did marry at quite a young age. Ebeneezer was several years older than I; that is the custom where I come from. Miletus is where Ebeneezer and I are from and where both of us were born, we had never been away from there until we left three years ago. I have a mother and two sisters there. My sisters, Tamara and Theta, have children of their own. I am the youngest in the family and it was very hard on my family for me to leave. But Ebeneezer had his eyes set on going and I, being the dutiful wife, was anxious to please him and go as well. I will be very anxious to be reunited with my family. It has been much too long since I have seen them and I know they will be thrilled to meet Julian." Tisha was so excited to tell her life story.

"They do know that Ebeneezer has passed on and that it happened very suddenly. One of the shepherds who I told you about was going to Miletus and I asked him to please locate my mother and let her and Ebeneezer's family know about his death. It would have been very hard on my husband's family to have received this news. I hated not being there to share with them in our time of mourning, but I could not do anything differently. I am certain they received the news and did not in any way blame me for not being able to have given him better care. When the fever strikes, there is not much that can be done. I kept him comfortable as well as I could and prayed that I or Julian did not contract it as well." The grief in Tisha's voice was hard to ignore.

"You do not have to tell me anymore. I know how difficult it is for you to talk about it. Whatever you want to say that gives you peace, it will be my pleasure to listen to, but please do not burden yourself unnecessarily." Onesimus was anxious to know all about Tisha as long as she was comfortable in sharing.

"My family does not know that we will be coming. It will be such a delightful surprise for them, I am sure. They will care for us as long as we need, and Julian and I will then make our place back in the community there. They are very active in the synagogue at Miletus and I will be treated as one of the widows for a while." Tisha suddenly realized what she had said. A widow in her mind had always been older ladies of the church who could not care for themselves. She had thought of them as helpless, deprived, and so alone. She wondered if that is how she would also be perceived by others.

"A synagogue? What is that? I have never heard that word before. And what do you mean 'will be treated as one of the widows'? How are they treated differently than how I am treating you now?" Onesimus was not shy to ask about things he had never heard.

"You do not know what a synagogue is? Where *are* you from that you do not have a synagogue? It is a place of worship. The community of believers gather together to worship God there. We look forward to the Sabbath day to study the Scriptures and get closer to God. Of course, only the men of the community really take part in any services. But in our town, the women are at least allowed to be there and glean from the reading of the Word. And for the question of how a widow is treated differently we have a time of mourning and during that period, the community helps out in every way necessary.

However, since I am under the age of 60, I am considered more able to care for myself after my period of mourning is over. But my family will support me, especially since I have a young child to care for. These are just traditions of the land and from the old law handed down to us." Tisha realized this was the first time she had ever had the opportunity of explaining traditions and anything of a spiritual nature to anyone.

"Well, the only kind of place of worship I have ever seen is the meeting in someone's home. Where I am from that was what happened. I thought that was the only time God's name was used. Anything else is new to me. Actually, as far as knowing what is to happen with a widow, I am at a loss since you are really the first one I have ever known." Onesimus realized he needed to guard what he said just in case he gave away too much of his past.

"That is enough of me for now. Let us talk about you and what plans you have. May I be so forward as to think that perhaps you are running away from something or somebody? Just remembering your appearance when I first saw you yesterday made me think that you were hiding from someone." Tisha could not hold back her anxiety any longer.

"I have no plans and no place to go. I guess you could say I am seeking a new life. I am pleased for the opportunity to accompany you to Miletus, wherever that is. By the way, do you have any idea how much further we have to travel before reaching our destination?" It really did not matter to Onesimus since his life was in Tisha's care, so to speak.

"It seems as though it took four days to get here when we came, but I cannot remember exactly and like I said, we were thrilled to be making the trip and did not have a child." Tisha had been noticing Onesimus periodically look over his shoulder and could not help but wonder why. "Is there something you are looking for? Sometimes you look a little jittery."

"Why? What do you mean? I am not looking for anything, really. I guess I have a habit of looking around. That is all." Onesimus did not realize it was obvious that he had been checking to see if anyone was following them. They were pretty much out in the open and could be spotted by the naked eye long before they could hear anyone come toward them.

"No problem. I suppose we each develop habits that we are not aware of until someone brings them to our attention." Onesimus was relieved that Tisha accepted his explanation.

"I do have a confession to make to you Tisha," Onesimus was a little embarrassed to share, "This is really the first time I have been around small children. Do you think Julian likes me?"

"I do believe that he does. So you have not been around widows, been to a synagogue, or been with small children. Just where have you been keeping yourself? You are too young to have been in prison." Tisha said jokingly not realizing how close she was to the real truth.

Chapter 6

Onesimus was amazed at how well he slept underneath the starry skies. He could not remember ever having slept out of doors in his entire life, even living as a slave. To him, the night was a very peaceful one after having gone to bed with the heavy feeling of guilt and remorse. So many thoughts kept running through his mind, especially that of having left his own mother who must be living in deep agony at this very moment. He reflected on what his father must be going through because he may very well have to answer for his own son's behavior. He was indeed anxious to know if his leaving had affected their safety. His mind could not help but think of Philemon, who was really a very good, kind man and Onesimus felt very badly for having hurt him this way. He remembered looking to the stars while he was counting his blessings for having gotten out of there, and before he knew it, the sun was up to welcome the morning.

It was a new day and he had to focus on the trip ahead and maintaining a good relationship with his new companions. After all, they could be his ticket out of all this. He continued to feel a sense of security with them by his side.

This second day of travel was quiet between Onesimus and Tisha. There was some concern in her mind about who he really was and where he came from. She would sure like to know more about her traveling companion. She was also thinking about the rugged trip ahead and not knowing exactly how long it would take. Tisha had hoped that Julian could have just strapped him on the donkey and travel this way. But to her regret, he had not been satisfied there, and either chose to try to walk along as the grownups or when that became tiresome he wanted to be carried. He was also used to a regular nap time. Thankfully, Julian had made a friend in Onesimus, and he was able to share in holding him.

As they traveled along the way, Tisha tried her best to dismiss the thought of robbers that might overtake them at any time. She very seldom had heard of anyone being attacked or robbed in this area but there was always the possibility. This was not a road frequently taken by people who would be transporting valuables.

Tisha knew that at the first opportunity, she would try to get Onesimus to open up to her. She did not want to be too presumptuous or do anything to scare him off. She knew more than anything she had ever known in her life that she desperately needed his help and she felt a lot safer with him around, although he was just a young fellow and appeared not to be very experienced in a lot of areas.

Evening finally came and Tisha just felt the need to get to know Onesimus a little better. She somehow felt drawn to him. She wondered if maybe it was his eyes because they looked so tender to her. She knew she could always tell the gentleness of a person by looking into their eyes and his looked very kind. "Ah, what sweet relief to be able to sit under the stars and enjoy the rest and be able to get off my feet. They feel as though they have gone more than 25 miles today. I am very impressed by the fire that you made for us so I could cook these lentils that I managed to pack. The nourishment from them will do us good. We really need to pace ourselves and not push so hard tomorrow." Tisha began rubbing her feet as she spoke, realizing that Onesimus had much more energy than she.

"Oh I am very sorry if I have pushed you to go at a heftier pace than you and Julian can handle. I forgot that you might not be as able to go my pace. I will be more aware of that tomorrow." Onesimus spoke as he was enjoying the food that Tisha had prepared.

"Please do not apologize. I know I do not have the energy that you have. We will be fine if we just take a few more rest stops tomorrow. I am very anxious to get to Miletus, but I do not want to be totally exhausted when we do." Tisha realized Onesimus was trying his best to be compliant, but knew he was feeling a little awkward with being around her as if he had never been with a female before. She thought it also seemed that he was in a hurry to move on for some reason.

"I fully understand. Please let me know when you need to stop and I most assuredly will be happy to take time out for a break. It will give me an opportunity to spend time with Julian. I look forward to playing with him in the open fields. A child such as he is really quite refreshing." Onesimus spoke with an excitement that Tisha had not seen before.

"I cannot wait to get to Miletus and see my family. As I said before, they have not had the opportunity to mourn the loss of Ebeneezer with me and that will mean so much to be able to just hold each other for a while. So if we push too hard our bodies will not make it tomorrow. Besides, having a child along makes a definite difference in speed." Tisha could not believe how tired she was yet she had so much enthusiasm in being able to share with Onesimus.

"I feel just as you do. I have been used to hard work my entire life and have constantly been on my feet most of the day, but this has been different. It is so relaxing to just rest under the stars. I have never felt such peace before. It is like I don't have a care in the world." Onesimus could not believe he actually felt that way. To think that only two days before, he had been running for his life.

"Onesimus, you seem like a fine young man. I am a good listener. If you ever want to talk about yourself, your family, your life, I would love to hear all about it."

"Let's just say I miss my mother and father that I left behind. I have never been apart from them. I feel that I will never see them again and that makes me very sad. My mother must be going through agony right now at the thought of my taking off." Onesimus was thinking out loud and hoping that his running away had not adversely affected the lives of his parents.

"You said 'taking off'. What did you mean by that? Who are you running from? If that is the case I am sure that your poor mother is quite worried about you." Tisha thought she had discovered a little of what was going on with him. She now had a clue.

Onesimus had to think fast. "What I meant was that I left at night. I took off after it got dark and she would be more concerned about my safety in going that time of day. Anyway, the worst part of the trip is not being able to be with her."

"I know what you mean. I have not seen my mother for so long. But if God is willing, I will arrive at her house day after tomorrow. Miletus, where my entire family lives, is a town where everyone knows each other. All my sisters and their children are there. I also have aunts and uncles and they have all lived in the same house their entire lives. I am the only one of my family who has ever left. Oh, I am sorry, I believe that I have told you that before. Please excuse me. It is just that I have not been with anyone for so long, it feels very good just to be able to have a conversation with another adult." Tisha realized she must be repeating herself, but with the excitement of the trip, she could not contain herself. "That is the only life I knew until I took off with Ebeneezer. Our parents arranged for our marriage and I was very pleased. I always had a fondness for Ebeneezer, even as a child. He was so playful. But Ebeneezer got the idea he wanted to be out from under the family and assert his independence. So we, being young and foolish, moved out here, claimed the land, and built our little house. We met some neighbors and had quite a few really good times here, but that is in the past now." There was sadness in her face as she thought of what could have been.

"Again, I did not want to make you sad. When you get to your family maybe you will have more joy in your heart." Onesimus knew he needed to cheer her up and even though she had pretty much shared this before, he realized she felt better saying it again. Somehow it made her feel closer to her husband and the life she had just left.

"Oh, I have joy inside all right. I have the peace and love of the Lord. Ebeneezer and I heard about Jesus and His power to save souls and rescue the needy. That is what I was when

Ebeneezer left me to go to heaven to be with Jesus. I was a very needy soul." Onesimus realized she was talking about something happy but was not sure at all what to make of it and since he was ready for a good night's sleep , he would let it go at that. He only wanted to reflect on the day and how he marveled at the countryside, the beautiful scenery he had only dreamed about, the few people they had met on the way, and oh yes, the freedom!

The days of being together proved to be very memorable for Onesimus. Being in the company of a female was something he was getting used to since his mother was the only female he had interacted with. They began to loosen up with each other and they even found themselves laughing together over the silliest things. This was good for Tisha also since she had been alone for so long, she had forgotten what laughter was like. Onesimus noticed there was something special about her, especially as he looked into her eyes as she talked. He also was taken in by her smile, making her face totally light up when she did so. There was a sparkle he never knew existed. He had never seen such radiance before and he had certainly never experienced the excitement that he felt while talking with her.

Onesimus had not spent much time with children and found out how much fun he had playing with Julian and helping in his care. When they took a break from their walking, Onesimus would swing Julian around in his arms, chase after him along the edge of a stream and splash a little water on him to make him laugh. He had never known the joy of being part of a family—a family blessed with freedom, that is.

They arrived in Miletus thrilled with the sight of so much activity in this busy little town. However, as Tisha had already explained to Onesimus, the town is in slight decline commercially due to the silting up of its waterway. Things were still very lively as far as Tisha was concerned since she had been in the wilderness for so long. Tisha found her mother and sister's home and Onesimus was touched by the embraces and tears of joy that greeted her there. It had been so long since this family had been together, and the reunion was wonderful to behold except, of course, in the absence of Ebeneezer. They were very excited to meet Julian and pledged to help in raising him. After all the enthusiasm died down, Tisha introduced Onesimus to them. He appeared to be a little shy when the formalities were exchanged, but they made him feel at home in no time.

After little response from the few questions of "Where are you going? Do you have someone in the area to see while you are here?" they agreed to allow Onesimus to stay with them.

Tisha's brother in law said there was room on the roof top and he could stay there for as long as he needed. Onesimus was quite relieved at that thought. He had feared that he was going to have to be on his own when he got to the town and he was actually dreading having to part with Tisha and Julian. He had never been on his own before and knew he was not prepared for looking for his own place or obtaining food to eat for that matter. He remembered that he had not had the opportunity to spend any of the money that he had stolen from Philemon, but also realized that it would not last too long if he had to use it to live on.

"Onesimus, here is a cover for you. I think you will find it very comfortable up here. This is the place we usually have visitors stay. We quite often have travelers visit because our home is always available to people we meet at the synagogue. Those folks that come to our church services are always very trustworthy and we feel safe in having them here. So you just make yourself at home here and we will have something put out on the table to eat in a little while." Tisha's sister was very kind and like no one he had ever met. She was very nice and he had trouble believing that she would be this hospitable to someone she had never seen before.

"Thank you so much. This will be just fine. I am very grateful for what you have provided for me. I will try not to be any trouble and will be happy to pay". Onesimus was touched by the gentleness of this stranger.

"Oh, no, it is I who should be grateful since you were able to help Tisha when she really needed someone. We hoped she would end up coming here but we were so worried about her making this trip all alone with Julian that we were beside ourselves. If only we had known that you were with her, we would have rested a lot easier. We did not know exactly when to expect them, but knew the time would come soon. We cannot begin to pay you back for your kindness to her." Tisha's sister showed her appreciation by fluffing up his bed a little more.

Chapter 7

fter a few days went by, Onesimus began feeling somewhat restless. For as long as he could remember, he had to work from daylight until dark and then some. However, since he had been in Miletus, he had his meals prepared for him, and nothing had been expected from him in return. He had been given a tour of the town by Jeremiah, to the point that he knew it very well and was amazed at how friendly all the people were. It was exciting for him to be living in a seaport town and enjoy some of the Greek culture. He had asked for chores to do or possibly repairs that needed to be made, but was always told that everything was going well. He knew it was time to start paying his own way since he was not used to having people provide for him, so he asked for suggestions on how he might find some sort of work. He explained to them how he had no training and did not know the culture of the area and that might make being hired a little more difficult. Tisha decided she would ask her sister, whose husband, Jeremiah, operated the boating system out of Miletus, to see if there was any opportunity for a position there.

When word got back to Onesimus that they needed a strong, energetic man to help with the ropes at the dock, he eagerly accepted the job. The position sounded as though it would need little training and he felt he could surely be capable of doing it. It was explained to Onesimus that he would need to sometimes ride from there to Cos and on to Rhodes to help with some deliveries. He had to hold back on how thrilled he really was. "I would actually be riding on a boat! I would relish the thought of having the opportunity to be on the water." In his wildest imagination, would he never have thought this would happen? He was comparing his excitement to the few times as a child when he would receive a gift such as a set of marbles at a birthday or be able to eat a special meal at a festivity where Philemon would have everyone join in. "Now those were the good times," he thought, as he reflected on his past.

Onesimus did turn out to be a very fast learner and actually enjoyed the work on the boat dock. He took great pleasure in the trips he had, especially the ones to Rhodes where he was introduced to some very tasty new foods including his favorite, Baklava. Onesimus delighted in viewing the Colossus of Rhodes. He would come home each night exhausted, but looked forward to another day of hard work and interacting with the pleasant men he worked alongside. He had been told that there was strife between the workers, who wanted a democracy, and the rich, who preferred a dictatorship. He remembered Tisha saying something about that and being one of the reasons Ebeneezer wanted to get away. Onesimus did not get involved in all of that, which made life a lot easier for him. He was thrilled to be able to share with Tisha all the experiences he was having. She enjoyed being a part of his enthusiasm that was so fresh and inspiring.

Upon reaching the docks early one morning and giving the boats a once-over to be sure everything was in place, he noticed the owner of all the boats was headed his way. Silas looked like he had something very important on his mind, and Onesimus wondered if he had done anything wrong.

"Onesimus, I have been watching your work over the last several weeks since you have been employed here, and I must say that I am very impressed with your abilities and dedication, My brother owns a line of boats, much larger than mine and I have received word that he is looking for someone to work for him. I wondered if you would be interested in that position. It would be a big advancement for you; however, you would need to move to Ephesus since that is where the work would be." Onesimushad heard that Ephesus was a major city of Greece and more prosperous as a commercial center, and he was eager to be able to go there as well. After all, he wanted to be adventuresome, and now he had that opportunity.

"That sounds very exciting. Thank you so much for offering me this chance for advancement. But move to Ephesus? I am not sure I could do that. May I have a day or so to think it through? The only drawback I can foresee would be in having to say good- bye to my new family." The reality of it all struck Onesimus, but when he found out it would be close enough to come back for visits, he was ready to accept.

"Please do not take too long since the boat that would take you there leaves day after tomorrow. You really do not want to miss this opportunity that may only come around once in your life." Onesimus could tell that Silas had his best interest at heart.

The time of leaving was very hard on all of them. Their new relationship had become deeply bonded but the time had come to part ways. Onesimus did not realize it would be so difficult to leave and the feeling was mutual with Tisha and all the others in her family. Onesimus promised to keep in touch and see them again as soon as he could.

After the 30- mile trip, he arrived in Ephesus where he met a different type of people from those he had been around in Miletus. Right away he realized he was in the company of more highly educated and worldly men who spoke of business matters and used terminology that he was not used to hearing. So he tried to make a good impression, but realized by now that people looked at him differently in this new world and he had to keep up if he was going to get anywhere here.

After a few weeks of being on the job, Onesimus knew his life was much better off now than it would have been if he had stayed around Colossae. He had no regrets for what he had done. His guilt of leaving had been dismissed from his mind for now, but he frequently thought of his mother and wondered how she was doing without him around to help her out. He had seen the temple of the goddess Diana and wondered what his mother would think of that. This life was not bad and the pay was pretty good, too. He had occasional time off and used it to buy nice things and enjoyed the new foods. "Yes," he thought, "this is indeed the good life."

"Onesimus, I would like to have a word with you." the captain of the boat called to him before returning to Ephesus.

He did not know what to think. He could not remember doing anything wrong. Maybe there was something he was supposed to do that he forgot. There is so much to remember that it could be he did not handle his job as well as he could have. This boat was quite a bit larger than the one he was originally trained on so maybe he did overlook something on that last trip. "Yes sir. Here I am. Please let me know if I have done anything that is displeasing to you. This is a little different boat than I was used to when I worked in Miletus. If you will be a little more patient with me I am sure that I will be able to manage my job."

"Oh, lad, it is nothing like that. You appear to have mastered this boat and look as though you have been a part of it for years. I was just going to tell you that I have been watching you and I am very impressed with your skills. You seem to get along really well with all the crew and that pleases me. Too often I get people in here that all they want to do is argue with everyone they meet. I spend more time breaking up fights that anything. No sir, you are exactly what I want and I just wanted to let you know that." Onesimus breathed a sigh of relief when his superior boasted of his qualifications.

"Thank you very much for your kind words, sir. I do appreciate the encouragement that you so freely give me." Onesimus was not used to people complimenting him and it felt very good.

After serving at the boat docks for a while, Onesimus was given the opportunity to take a load of people across the big waters to Athens. He jumped at this new opportunity. It bothered him, though, that he did not get the chance to go down to Miletus to tell Tisha and her family that he would be going so far away.

Wow! For a while he could see no land–only water for miles. This was quite different than anything he could have ever imagined in his lifetime. "Oh, if only father could be here; he would absolutely be overwhelmed as well," Onesimus thought he realized this must be what the heaven he had heard about would be like. How glorious. "The gods were surely looking out for him now" he thought, as he admired the beautiful blue waters of the Aegean Sea.

"You know if you keep up the good work, you may even be asked to take a load to Alexandria. That is the big shipping headquarters now and you would be able to see the largest ships that ever sailed the seas right there. Yes sir, that is a sailor's dream to go there and see all those fine ships come in and out of that port." Onesimus could tell that the captain knew what he was talking about and Onesimus would value that opportunity if it ever came his way. He had come to understand that when they referred to ships, they would be talking about much larger vessels than the smaller ones they called boats.

Onesimus enjoyed working with this crew just as well as before. They were all very polite and seemed to take him under their wing. Most of the men he had worked with so far were quite a bit older than he was. They were all seasoned and were able to show Onesimus many pointers 'of the sea'. He had learned to recognize the clouds and when severe weather would be a threat and to allow time if they could to avoid potential storms. He had learned to tie various knots and understand terms about the physical structure of the boat. It had even been explained to him to watch for the season of the year because leaving out as winter approached could prove to be very treacherous.

Over the months, Onesimus made several trips back and forth to Athens. However, there came a day when he decided he wanted more. If he was going to really see things, he wanted to do just that. He asked the captain of the ship if he could possibly have a different schedule. He assured him that he did not mind the hard work; after all, he had done that his whole life and compared to the kind of life his father and his father before him had had, this was not that bad at all.

One day not long after that conversation, he was told that he would be able to take a ship load of statues and ornamental displays to Rome across the Great Sea. He remembered hearing some of the men at Athens talk about the beautiful city of Rome "To think, I would have the advantage to explore the whole world! It is not Alexandria as I hoped it would be, but still a great place to go" Onesimus thought. He was told to think very carefully about this. The seas could be quite dangerous and he would be on the water for weeks. He did not have to think twice. Onesimus accepted this assignment quite readily.

Chapter 8

The sky was bright and the winds were calm. A great day for sailing. Onesimus was a well-seasoned seaman by now. He had not ever felt the least bit seasick as had been the experience of some of the other men with whom he had sailed. He had heard many stories of men who were so sick they had to be taken off never to set sail again. Since he showed all the traits of a true sailor, he had been given many opportunities. So this was a new adventure for Onesimus. How exciting the thought of being able to sail to Rome and to cross the Mediterranean Sea. He kept thinking how far he had advanced and how many advantages had come his way.

He was very anxious to meet the crew with whom he would be working, after all, he had gotten along very nicely with everyone so far and had learned very much from each of them. He anticipated that this trip and new ship would be no different. He was ready to start out on this momentous voyage. But his expectations were not met. Soon after they set sail, he realized he was in the midst of a hostile environment. The men he would be sailing with for the next several weeks were quite angry with the world and used language that he had never heard before. Not even among the men of Ephesus he worked with, had he ever encountered such antagonism. Onesimus could live with unfriendliness, but the verbal abuse he had to work with was unthinkable. Most of the men were very rough and crude to him and anyone who got in their way better watch out.

"Hey you, pick up that anchor and throw it in the water for me, will you?" a big robust, smelly man told Onesimus very harshly.

Onesimus was not familiar with that term, but he knew it could not be good. He, too, wanted to act very tough but did not have it in him. All he could think of was the fear that had overtaken his entire being.

"What am I going to do?" Onesimus asked himself. "That anchor is much bigger and heavier than I am. There is no way I am able to pick it up by myself, much less throw it overboard into the water." And what Onesimus had trouble understanding was the thought that they knew he could not physically do it.

All Onesimus could hear was laughter. There was a circle of men around him. He was looking up at much larger men than he had ever seen before. And the anger in their faces was really frightening to Onesimus. The stench radiating from their bodies was very nauseating to Onesimus. He wondered when the last time was any of them had taken a bath. All of them were laughing at him. Onesimus could never remember being so humiliated. They were spitting at him and kicking the anchor at him. Some were yelling out profanities and calling him names he had never heard before but he was sure they were far from kind.

"I don't see why you expect me to pick the anchor up. It is not just my job to do it, but this is to be teamwork. We are supposed to work together, you know." Onesimus tried to say this in a strong voice, but knew it sounded very weak and feeble. He knew that from having worked on the smallest boat to the largest ship that everyone pulled their own weight and worked together. When someone had difficulty in their assigned task, there would always be another to help out. But not in this case. Onesimus was certainly caught by surprise.

"Look who we have to work with now. A little weakling has arrived. Just you be sure we are not picking up your slack." One of the men jeered.

"Okay break it up, break it up," Onesimus heard an authoritative voice say. "They are just trying you. They are testing you to see what you are made of. If they ever cause you any more problems, you be sure and come to me," an even bigger, burlier man announced as Onesimus got up watching two or three of the men toss the anchor overboard. Onesimus was so thankful for this man and knew he would try to stick close to him during the entire trip.

After a few days on the sea, Onesimus decided to look around the ship a little bit. He was feeling quite homesick by now. For the first time since he had left Philemon's house, he had the feeling of wanting to be somewhere else. He could not actually pinpoint it if it was home in Colossae or could it be he was really missing Tisha?

He had never been on a ship quite this large before, but began to feel confident enough in himself and secure in the thought that if those brutes bothered to ask where he was going, he could handle himself enough that it would not be a problem. He knew that if he kept to the task assigned to him, there should not be any reason for controversy.

After taking a turn or two around the lower level of the ship, he thought he heard voices. He could not at first believe his ears because amazingly enough what he heard was laughter. This was something he had not experienced since he had left Ephesus. As he got closer, he had been spotted before he was able to observe where the laughter came from. One of the two men asked him to come in to what appeared to be a place where food would be prepared. He knew that he had been fed pretty well since he had been on this ship, but had not thought about where it came from. The shorter of the two men stretched out his hand and introduced himself as Agus and he was told that the other was named Credo. They seemed quite different than any of the others on board. Their duties had been to see that the rest of the crew were fed. They had a gentle nature, and he realized that these qualities were more to his liking. He had never before in his lifetime been exposed to the cruelty and vulgarity used by the others and he was quite anxious for a change in attitude.

"You are new to the crew here aren't you?" one of Onesimus's newfound friends asked him. He realized he felt really comfortable with them.

"Yes, I had been working on ships in the Ephesus area and was given the opportunity to sail the high seas and go to places I never knew existed. I eagerly waited for the day when this would happen so I knew I could not turn it down," Onesimus said realizing he now had someone he could share his thoughts with.

"Then why do you look so sad, you should feel more excited to have what you always wanted? You have very sorrowful eyes, if I may say so," Agus said.

"It is the other men up there. They treat me worse than a slave. I cringe every time I come close to any of them. They put the fear in me from the very first day I came on board," Onesimus said very quietly just in case the wrong person was listening in.

"We understand fully what you are going through. There would be no way either of us could possibly work in those conditions. We have often wondered why the crews crossing over to Rome have always been so rough. It is like the big seas bring out the worst in these men. We are both so glad we are able to stay down in the galley and do our work and not have to deal with anyone else. We certainly keep our distance, and we feel sorry for you due to the fact that you cannot get away from them." Credo spoke very assuredly.

"I am not used to people who are so harsh. My whole life I thought I had it really bad, but I realize now that I had been sheltered from the world. I have seen more and been exposed to more things in the last few months than I could have ever dreamed possible. My world as I knew it was really very gentle and peaceful. I had people around who truly loved me and my working conditions I realize now were not all that bad. Sure I had to constantly take orders and was trapped in a small part of the world, but as my father and mother always told me 'it could certainly be a lot worse'. I may be finding that out right now." Onesimus could not believe he had been so open with these two men who he had just met. Suppose what he had just said got back to the others? What if they find out he was a slave and had run away? Surely, he did not want the others to find out. If he was being treated so roughly now, he could only imagine how it would be then.

"You know that your strength has come from the touch of the Lord's hand to be able to have endured it all. He has protected your young life and directed you on the straight path." Agus spoke with authority as if he understood Onesimus's heart.

"I don't know anything about that. I only know that my life has taken a change in a direction that I have not enjoyed ever since I left for this trip." Onesimus was not sure at all what Agus was talking about.

"Jesus is what gets us through each and every day. We just do our jobs and try to live a good example and maybe it will pay off. Perhaps even one of the crew will understand the gospel and it will be worth it. Credo and I are brothers in the Lord and we only took this position because the pay is good and we have families to support in Delphi." Agus was hoping that he and his new friend Onesimus would have this common bond.

"What you say sounds really good, but I am afraid I am not following you at all. The only brothers I know of are those born to the same father and mother, and I am the only child my parents have. Well, my mother did give birth to another. He would have been two years older than me, but he died. I never did know any more about how that happened." Onesimus tried to join in the conversation the best way he knew how considering he did not know what they were talking about, although he had heard bits and pieces while with Tisha's family. "I certainly do not know about being an example to anyone." Onesimus spoke looking quite confused.

"Tell us, what brought you down here? It is no accident that you found us." Credo said hoping that they were not scaring him off.

"Oh I was just doing some exploring around. But you know, I have heard some mention about this Jesus. Could it be the same one that Tisha spoke of?" Onesimus was thinking out loud.

"Who is Tisha, you wife?" Agus asked but thought that he looked a little young to be a family man.

"Tisha was my traveling companion from just west of Colossae. We spent some time on the road together. Then I stayed at her family's home in Miletus while I worked for their family's boating business there. That is where I got introduced to working on boats, but on a much smaller scale." It was obvious that Onesimus brightened up when he mentioned Tisha's name.

"Oh, I see, a traveling companion, eh? Could there be a little more to the relationship?" Credo knew he would get a smile out of Onesimus and it worked.

"Please, forgive me, I have not told you my name. It is Onesimus. I am honored to meet the two of you." Onesimus was embarrassed that he had shared so much about himself but had neglected to introduce himself.

"We are glad to meet you, Onesimus, and hope that this is the first of many visits we may have together. You are different than all the others and we would take joy in having you around. It sometimes gets pretty lonely with just the two of us to keep company together." Credo spoke with a big smile showing that he had two front teeth missing.

"We also miss being with our families while we are gone for such a long span of time in making these extended trips across the seas. I have three children and a wife back in Delphi. There is not much work available there especially that pays what I get doing this. I have always enjoyed indulging in food, so this was the best way I could provide for my family and keep my stomach filled at the same time." Credo spoke in a spirit that was becoming contagious to Onesimus.

"This is not a bad life. No indeed. I, too, have a family in Delphi. I have always been interested in sailing, but never thought I had the strength to pull my weight on the seas. So, since I too, enjoy eating, I hooked up with Credo and we became a team. My wife died not too long ago, though, from sores that had come up all over her body. Her mother and the rest of her family take care of my two sons while I am away.

They do a very good job with them, but I do miss them while I am gone. When I am home, it is usually for a month. So that gives us good time together." Agus spoke as though he was proud of his family but saddened at the thought of having lost his wife.

"I am very sorry for your loss, Agus, but know that you enjoy being with your sons while you are home." Onesimus wanted to be sure Agus and Credo knew that he took interest in their lives.

""Thank you. I appreciate your kindness," Agus spoke realizing he had not been used to this kind of sincerity on the ship.

"Yes, I would love to spend time with you. May we get together when my turn is over from up on deck? I would love to hear more." Onesimus was somewhat interested, but his main objective was just to be able to carry on a conversation with some kind, gentle people while keeping his distance from the others.

Chapter 9

Later, after the sun went down and everything seemed calm on the waters Onesimus knew his work was done for the day. He went below to seek out Credo and Agus and found Agus reading aloud to Credo. Onesimus was intrigued and sat in the background to just listen for a while. It felt really good to sit and relax because all the bones in his entire body ached. Since he did not have the ability to read or had heard very little from any kind of written word, he just settled himself back and listened. He was learning about a man named Abraham and something about God's chosen people.

He thought he would just sit quietly, but before he knew it, he had been spotted by Credo who welcomed him with a smile. "Good to have you join us. We had just wondered if we would be seeing you this evening."

"I overheard you reading something about God choosing people for His very own. Is that really true? If indeed you believe for yourself what you are reading, then please explain it to me as that is a new concept to me. What is it that you are reading anyway? I actually am just so impressed to know someone who can read so well." Onesimus was indeed very interested..

"Greetings, Onesimus. It is so good to see you again. What I am reading is called the Scriptures. This was actually written hundreds and hundreds of years ago. I am not sure when, but what is important is what is in it. If you would like, you can stay with us for a while and listen. This is what we do each evening. We work so hard during the day that we look forward to this time each night. We take turns reading the Torah and you are most welcome to join us." Agus was excited to be able to include someone in their little circle.

"I would be so happy to be a part of this. Please under-stand though that I would not be able to contribute anything. Reading is one thing that I have never been taught, nor have I even seen anything written before. On occasion, I had the habit of enjoying the readings of some elders in the community. I was always fascinated by what came out of those parchment papers they read from. I do not recall much of what they said, but at the time I remember finding it quite enlightening. If I truly may, I will be here each evening after I put in my day's work." Onesimus once again chose to be a part of this group just to be around friendly people and away from the others. He was very excited at the prospect that perhaps he could broaden his horizons and this would be far better than being alone feeling so depressed.

Each day Onesimus would arise before the sun came up and begin his day of rigorous labor on the upper level of the ship, all the while dealing with the obnoxious and brutal men who worked next to him. He managed to keep a low profile and realized that the less contact he had with them, the better off he was. He, too, found that he was looking forward to each evening when he had the opportunity to hear from the Word as he learned to call it. It was becoming much more than a diversion from either being alone or keeping distance from the other men. He sensed he was being drawn to the Word of God. "Amazing that I would ever feel this way about stories out of the Scriptures. To think I never knew it even existed a few weeks ago; now it is a part of my life," he said to himself as he headed down to where his quarters were in order to freshen up a little before heading to what had become his evening ritual.

Agus and Credo read to Onesimus from David's Psalms and how we should be joyful when we don't really feel that way and that our strength comes from the Lord. He is truly our rock that we can stand upon. Onesimus just had a flash from the past of the times he would sneak peeks at the assembly that gathered in Philemon's home and read from a tablet just like this. He understood now that they were also reading from God's Word. Could that be true? Yes, he realized now that the group that so faithfully met in his master's home were godly men who chose to take time out from their very busy days to join together and learn from God's Word. The man up front who was doing most of the talking was the one who was teaching it all to them.   No wonder they always seemed to be in good spirits and greeting even the servants with compassion. It was all coming together now.

It got to the point that Agus and Credo were showing him the words as they were reading them and before long, Onesimus's quick mind was picking out some of the phrases. His eyes followed along as they ran their finger over the words as they were being read and they made it come alive to him. He found he was becoming challenged, and this was very exciting to him to actually be able to read the Word of God for himself. He remembered hearing Archippus read aloud to the group that met in Philemon's house and how astounded he was to think of people being able to do that. And now, Onesimus could be counted among those who were able to read. "Wouldn't mother be so proud of me now, if only she knew?"

He was especially delighted in David's son, Solomon, and all the wisdom that God had given him with the Proverbs. He enjoyed the part about a woman named Ruth who left her family to live in a distant land and established the line of David. He could certainly relate to leaving his homeland and family to go off to a faraway place. They taught him about Noah and how his obedience had saved him and his family from the flood and destruction. He was finding that obedience to the God of these Scriptures was so important in the life we live. Credo said that most important of all was where the Scriptures talked of someone coming who would be a king who would rule over all the people.

Onesimus took delight in passages such as Isaiah saying "I am the first and I am the last, apart from me there is no God." That had such impact on Onesimus's view of the Almighty as Agus seemed to always refer to Him. Also in Isaiah: "Our Redeemer–the Lord Almighty is his name, is the Holy One of Israel." Onesimus reflected "I am finding so much on these pages that appear to be making a difference in my life."

"So this points to someone who, at that point in the writing, had not yet come. How exciting to think of people writing about things that had not yet occurred," Onesimus never ceased to be amazed at what was disclosed by reading from God's Word.

"Anything you are able to tell me is good enough for me. Whatever I can fill my head with to get away from the nonsense that comes from those brutal men upstairs is fine with me." Onesimus agreed with all that Agus and Credo told him, just because it sounded good enough to him.

Chapter 10

As the ship began to draw near to the pier, all the crew had to do their part in getting the cargo unloaded. After that was accomplished, Onesimus looked around and found Agus and Credo waiting for him a little way down the road. "You know we have to walk a ways to be able to get to the heart of the city." Onesimus had thought he would be in the city of Rome as soon as he got off the ship.

"Oh, I do not mind a little walk on dry ground after having been on board that ship for so long."

Onesimus was actually startled by the magnitude of the city of Rome and how the buildings and houses he saw were so spread out. As far as his eye could see, the city rolled on and on. Until working with the men in Ephesus, Onesimus had never known such a place had existed, and he was remembering that those men with whom he had worked used to tell stories among themselves of how it was always bustling with activity. He was trying to recall some of the things he had overheard the men from Athens tell of their trips to Rome. They would make this city sound like a fabulous place to be as they raved over its enormity, artistry, and culture. He was told that it was a very large city but he had not envisioned how extraordinarily big it really was. Everywhere he looked were people walking around, carrying packages; there were markets all over the place displaying all sorts of pottery, fine linens, and jewelry. It seemed like all nations and people from everywhere in the world were represented here. Onesimus had been familiar with soldiers riding on horses as they patrolled the countryside, but here they appeared much larger and so much more intimidating as they rode down the streets with all their pomp and splendor. They were very overwhelming with the armor they had on that appeared way too heavy for their bodies to carry. He was almost blinded by the flash that came from their long, dangerous-looking swords as they made contact with the sun's rays.

He could hear various languages being spoken and won-dered if he would have a difficult time being able to communi-cate while he was here. He found himself staying very close to Credo and Agus since they appeared to know where they were going and seemed a lot more confident than he was. Onesimus was afraid to say anything fearing that if someone recog-nized his accent, he might be found out and turned over to the authorities. Onesimus constantly wished he could put his past behind him and just move on with a new life without the constant guilt and fear of being caught, imprisoned, or worse.

"What are we going to do with ourselves now that we are here? We have a whole week before the ship departs again." Onesimus felt insecure and hoped Agus and Credo were not planning on abandoning him any time soon. "I know nothing of this place. I know no one, have no idea where to go, what is safe, or who to trust.".

"Do not worry, Onesimus, we will not leave you, if that is what you are concerned about," Credo spoke up, realizing how overcome with anxiety Onesimus must be.

"We know where we can rent a room. It is the same place we always go when we come to Rome. The people who own the place pretty well keep up with our schedule and we can count on them to hold rooms for us. We can see if they will be able to put you up as well. You got paid quite adequately for the work you did on the ship in coming here, did you not?" Agus asked hoping for Onesimus's sake that he would be willing to go with them.

"For lack of anywhere else to go, I would love to be your companion. I really want to continue our relationship. I have come to depend on the two of you for so many things and could not imagine not having you with me through the next few days. I admit that I would be really afraid without your leadership after what I have seen so far." Onesimus's fear turned to glee as he picked up his belongings and headed out with the two after they motioned for him to follow them.

After walking along several streets, they turned into the entrance of a wide open door that brought them to a little inn. It was far from fancy, in fact it was very plain, but it appeared to be clean and inviting. Credo and Agus were greeted very enthusiastically by a small- framed man with a beard. After the formalities, Agus introduced Onesimus to him as their new brother. Onesimus was always taken aback when he heard this expression, but at that moment, it did not bother him at all. He was actually quite elated that they had developed that kind of relationship with him which he had never had with anyone before. The next thing he knew, he had been handed a very large key that he assumed was to a room that would be his for at least that night. Onesimus had never used a key to open a door before. In fact everywhere he had ever been, there was never that kind of security. Onesimus was surprised to find out that there were rooms available for each of them to lodge in for the entire week while in Rome waiting for their return trip to Athens. Onesimus would have been just as happy to share the room with his new friends, but these arrangements were fine with him. The room assigned to Onesimus was very little consisting only of a small bed and a table with an oil lamp on it. That was all he really needed anyway. At least he had his own privacy which was more than he was accustomed to. While living on the roof of Tisha's family's home, people were always coming and going.

As Onesimus was looking out his small window to see what he could see down below, he heard a knock at his door. "Would you like to go to the market down the street and get something to eat? I don't know about you but I am very hungry." Realizing Onesimus was looking sad, Credo asked, "What is wrong, is there something I can do for you?"

"Oh, I was just thinking how overwhelming this all is and how different this way of life is than what I would have ever thought possible. And wishing that my father and mother could be able to have just a little taste of what I have experienced over the last several months. You know, they never went anywhere outside of the farm they lived on. Even now to be here in Rome and take in just a little part of what it has to offer is very overwhelming to me," Onesimus explained. He realized he was somewhat homesick.

"You are just tired and hungry. Let us go check out the food here. At least it will be better than the stuff you have been fixing back on the waters, Credo," Agus enjoyed joking with Credo every chance he got.

"You will be your cheery self before long," Credo assured Onesimus as they headed down the stairs and turned left toward the markets.

Onesimus found that he had to almost turn sideways as he walked along to be able to fit through all the crowds of people walking in the street. Everyone seemed to be in a very big hurry, unlike the smaller towns and communities he had been used to. In his more familiar setting the people ambled along and managed to speak to the people they met along the way and were not nearly so rude.

They bought their food from some sort of slanted stand and after paying for it they found a table and began eating the most delicious corncakes Onesimus had ever had. After pointing out a few of the highlights, they were able to, they were joined by two men who seemed to be known by both Agus and Credo. "May we join you?" asked the men who greeted Agus and Credo with a large embrace and kiss. That was interesting for Onesimus to observe–two grown men hugging and kissing each other on the cheek.

"So you just arrived in the city? There have been some uprisings of late. You need to be very careful what you say and who you say it to. Things have tightened up recently. You may have noticed more of the horsemen and armored military men walking around. The Christians are in more danger than they have ever been." Broasso spoke very matter of factly to Agus and Credo.

"I was afraid that would happen. As if it were not already bad enough. What has happened to make them tighten up?"

Credo was very interested in knowing about the change of events.

"You are familiar with the witness of Paul of Tarsus. Well, he is in Rome now, but is under house arrest. He has gotten things a little stirred up. But on the positive side of that, you are here in what I would consider perfect timing. You might just be able to see him in person. So if you are not too tired, I have a real surprise for you. Paul is preaching in his home– well not the home of his choice, but rather where he has been assigned, shall we say. Anyway in just about an hour from now he will be speaking. We were on our way there and knew that if we ran across anyone who might be interested in hearing him, we would be sure to let them know so they could attend. We would be so pleased if you would join us. He would be very delighted to have you there." Broasso gave out his invitation very enthusiastically in hopes they would accept.

"Who do we have here? I do not believe I have had the pleasure of your acquaintance," one of the very nice men said.

"This is Onesimus. He was working on the ship with us that just brought over all the statues and pretty things from Athens. He is an extremely hard worker and has a very kind and gentle spirit. I believe he said he was from the area of Colossae, is that right Onesimus?" Credo took pride in introducing him to his friends.

Onesimus got up to shake hands with the men, but they did not extend their hands to him; instead, they gave him a brotherly embrace taking Onesimus completely off guard, but he accepted their gesture.

"Yes, that is right, I am from Colossae. My family is still there, but I was ready to be out on my own and find out how the rest of the world lived," Onesimus replied, choosing his words carefully.

"We would be pleased if you could accompany us down the street to where Paul will be speaking. You probably have not heard of him, but that is all right. You will feel that you know him very well after today. The day is still young, so how about coming along with us?" asked the man who had introduced himself as Marcus. The men were trying their best to get a crowd of people to be in attendance at this assembly.

Onesimus was really tired and all he wanted to do was go up to bed and take in a good rest; however, he was not really ready to be alone in such a terrifying place. "Oh yes, I would be honored to accompany you to this meeting. I will be ready whenever you are," he answered them.

When they got to the door of the house, Onesimus realized that it was not a very large place, but when they went inside he was amazed to be escorted to a courtyard where many people were already assembled. The focus of attention was on a small-framed man who appeared to be in his sixties but he could not say for sure. Whatever his age, he was still very spry. The men took a seat on the ledge of the open window area and after everyone was in place, Paul began speaking. As he did so, a quietness spread throughout the courtyard. His voice was strong, vivacious and what he had to say was so interesting that Onesimus was mesmerized instantly. Paul spoke of the faith of Abraham–one of the men Onesimus had read about in the Scriptures while on the ship with Credo and Agus. He talked about righteousness and how wonderful he made it sound. He then spoke of another man, David, whom they had read about being a man after God's own heart, but Paul made these Scriptures so alive. He spoke with authority in a way that Onesimus had never heard, and he had very great understanding of the Word.

"Credo." Onesimus quietly said to him with a look of wonderment. "I am really enjoying listening to him. Does he always speak with such great knowledge and comprehension of the words that we read about in the Scriptures?"

"Always," Credo answered on seeing that Onesimus was impressed. "He has been given a special gift of the Holy Spirit to know the Scriptures, to exhort them and to speak in such a tender yet bold enough way that the listener hangs on to every word. He has been empowered with God's wisdom to share with what God's plan is."

"How long does he usually speak? When I came in here, I was very tired and all I wanted to do was sleep, but now I am so engrossed with what he is saying that I feel I could listen to him for hours and hours." Onesimus was so glad he had come and not given in to his own desires and gone to bed.

"Paul has been known to speak all evening and way up until noon the next day. People continue to want to hear more, and Paul never runs out of tremendous things to say. The crowds just continue to get larger. Have you noticed? People are hungry for the Word; Jews and Gentiles alike, Of course here you will notice it is Gentile country, and they are the people Paul was called to minister to anyway." Credo was even more excited that Onesimus was enthralled. He was thinking and praying all the time he was talking that there could be a new brother in the Lord in the making.

After Paul's stimulating message and question after question being asked from his audience, everyone took a break, but were encouraged to not go too far because Paul would be continuing with his message soon.

Onesimus could not help but ask of Credo and Agus, "Have either of you met Paul? I mean have you spoken with him personally? It would be such a privilege to be able to actually talk with him. For a common man to really be able to get close and carry on a conversation with him would be amazing."

"No, never have we had that honor of personal contact with him. I would love the opportunity to speak with him one on one, but as you see here, he always has people around him. While they are in his presence, they want to make their time his time. I cannot imagine the stamina he has to speak forth the Word as he does and still be able to have people gather round and talk with him hours on end. He is a very special person, yes indeed. But he does not want you to think of him as anyone great. He considers himself the 'least of the least'." Agus assured Onesimus that Paul was approachable and it was just a matter of being able to get to him through all the others.

"I would like that opportunity to learn at his feet. You have been so wonderful to make the Scriptures known to me for the very first time. But now, after listening to him, I can see that I need more than just reading. I am hungry to know more, much more in the way that Paul described it all." Onesimus was using such dramatic body language as he spoke that he actually got Paul's attention from across the room.

"Please tell me what the situation is with Paul living here. I gathered that something was a bit unusual about what was going on here," Onesimus asked.

"We must have overlooked all the details in our anxiousness to get here. Apparently this house has been provided for Paul by some of his followers. They made sure he had an adequate place to stay so he did not have to live in a place, shall we say, not fit for the rats that would be in residence there. He has not been in Rome very long, but he is currently under house arrest. It is with our understanding that he usually is in chains, but today he is being watched very carefully. See the guards over there? He got special permission to walk around freely today and be able to speak to the crowd. It seems that a decree from Claudius has elapsed and more Jews have returned to Rome with their leaders. In order not to have an immediate upset, they decided to allow Paul the pretense of more liberty. Even so, they see Paul as a troublemaker." Agus had heard rumors about Paul being in trouble, but was hesitant to give Onesimus too much information since he seemed so inspired by the teachings of Paul. He did not want to do anything at this point to take away from his enthusiasm.

"Troublemaker — what do you mean by that? He appears to be such a tender-hearted man. I cannot think of him causing any trouble. Please tell me about his trouble." Onesimus would not take no for an answer and was very adamant about knowing everything there was to know about this new-found scholar.

"It is not that he has done anything wrong. It is just that the leaders have stirred up things against him because of exactly what he is doing now, except he was doing it in the streets, the synagogues, and I understand the Temple in Jerusalem, and his testimony preceded him wherever he went. They had warned him to not talk about this new King. The One we acknowledge as Savior. But he would not stop. And short of being selfish, we are so glad he did not quit. If it was not for his continuation, we would not have the knowledge that we do have about the Savior. He just explains things so well that our hearts and minds absorb the teachings so clearly. But we do not have the ability to teach like he does." Credo tried to explain to Onesimus as best he could but he also did not understand the magnitude of why Paul did not have the liberty to say what he needed to.

The room once again became quiet and Paul resumed his message. He gave it all he had because he knew his time was limited and this could be the only opportunity he would have to relate to a lot of the people here. After a little longer, it was apparent that Paul was totally exhausted, and he bid the crowd farewell. However, that was not enough for Onesimus.

"Do you mind staying around a little longer? I just have to at least give my greetings to Paul. I would not be able to sleep tonight if I did not come face to face with him and tell him how much I learned and how I appreciate his willingness to share with us." Onesimus so hoped they would be willing to wait because he sure did not want to walk down the street by himself, especially at this hour.

"I do not know if that is a good idea, Onesimus. You can see how tired Paul appears. If each of us that really wanted to talk personally with him, did so, it would take days. You can see for yourself how he needs to get his rest." Credo thought he had convinced Onesimus when a surprising thing happened.

The three men could not help but notice that Paul was actually making his way right toward where they were standing.

"Young man, my eyes could not help but notice you from the distance. I was encouraged by your enthusiasm. There was just something about you that drew me to come to you and speak." Paul acknowledged Onesimus.

"Me, do you mean me?" Onesimus hesitantly asked this highly esteemed man.

"I do not believe we have met, but I did observe that you were really absorbing the message. Have you been in the Word long?" Onesimus was very greatly taken aback by the fact that Paul had approached him first. What a testimony!

"No, we have never met. I just arrived in Rome today, and this is my first time to be here. I never knew of you until this very evening and I must say that I was really stirred by your message." Onesimus found his voice quivering as he spoke.

"Your accent tells me that you may be from Asia Minor. I spent quite a lot of time in that area and the speech there is very distinct. Would I be correct in presuming so?" Paul lit up at the thought of making a connection from someone of the area he so deeply loved.

"I am actually from a small town in the Asian area. Probably you have not heard of it before," Onesimus said. He was really hoping that Paul had never heard of his little town because he was suddenly feeling very uncomfortable at the thought of bringing anything about his hometown up in conversation.

"Well, tell me son. I am very familiar with all the towns through there, great or small. The knowledge that I would meet someone from the area I loved so much is exciting to me." Onesimus realized as Paul spoke that he did indeed need to open up.

"It is Colossae in Phrygia. I lived there my whole life before the opportunity came available for me to sail the great seas. Yes, that is where I am from. But I have been gone for some time now. My family is still there though." Onesimus did feel more at ease now after having owned up as to where he was from.

"Well, I certainly do know about Colossae. Yes, indeed. I made many visits to Ephesus and that is not far away. I met a man named Epaphras. Such an energetic man for the Lord. He was so full of the spirit and wanted very badly to continue the work I had begun while in Ephesus. I never seemed to have the opportunity to go to Colossae, but Epaphras was instrumental in seeing to it that the Word of the Lord was spread there. I know you are young, but could you possibly have known of

Epaphras?" Paul was genuinely interested in finding out about the connection Onesimus might have.

"I think that name does sound familiar. Epaphras does sound like someone I heard of as being a leader in a group of men who met to study from the Word of God. I was not in actual contact with him though, so I cannot say I really knew him." Again, Onesimus found himself very uncomfortable in knowing what to say.

"That is too bad, for I would like to hear more about what is going on there. To know how the church is growing is very important to me. He had such enthusiasm, and he was one of the first from that area to take my message on to other places where I had not personally been. His ministry has been so crucial to me." Paul spoke with glee in his eyes at the thought of a new relationship with someone who could bring him up-to-date on what was of deep interest to him

"I really do not have much to offer you since I was not a part of his life nor was my father." Onesimus was trying his best to move the conversation on to a new topic.

"I am so glad to have the opportunity to know you, kind teacher, but my companions are waiting for me and it is really late. We are all very tired, including you, I am sure. Thank you for your teaching and maybe I can return again." Onesimus could not wait now to get out of there and away from Paul.

He felt really trapped and did not want to explain himself to such an upright and honorable person.

Paul sensed his urgency to leave and discerned that there was much more to the story, especially since Onesimus avoided answering some of the pertinent questions that Paul had asked. "Please feel free to come here any time. I am not going anywhere. Be assured that I mean you no harm in any way and want to be able to talk with you in depth. I believe that I really need to speak to you more about God's word and its meaning for you in your personal life. Will you please come back tomorrow?"

Onesimus wondered what he should do; what should he say to Paul? But before he knew it, the words came out of his mouth like he could not control them. "Yes, I would be honored to come back tomorrow if it pleases you."

"I did not get your name," Paul inquired.

"It is Onesimus" he said reluctantly. "I will see you tomorrow morning." Onesimus was wondering why Paul was so drawn to him.

"Maybe soon I will understand why" he thought as he looked around. Everyone had left the premises. A guard came over and placed the chains around Paul's ankles and he headed toward his bed.

"I cannot believe this. I just cannot imagine why Paul would have come over to you and made special contact in the midst of all the others there. What did he see in you that stood out, I wonder?" Credo was quite envious, but wanted to be sure Onesimus knew how very vital this connection would be to him.

"We trust that you realize how special this is for you. To be able to actually have a conversation with Paul, and for him to invite you back and speak with him further. I am very proud of the way you handled yourself with him, Onesimus." Agus, too, shared in the delight of the time spent with Paul.

Onesimus appreciated their encouragement and felt as though his feet were not touching the ground as he went home quite excited that he would have the opportunity to see Paul again tomorrow. He realized that this evening he had already learned so much and could not wait until the next morning to be able to continue,

"Tonight the Scriptures have been opened to me in such a way that I never thought possible. I can hardly wait until tomorrow when I will again see Paul," Onesimus shared with his new friends.

"We cannot blame you. This is an opportunity you do not want to miss out on" Agus stated as they approached the door leading to Onesimus's room.

As Onesimus settled down in his bed, he could not control the thoughts that went through his head. If Paul knew his Master–Philemon, would he soon realize that he was a runaway? Had Paul already spoken to Philemon and known that there was a slave that had left him? Would he soon find out that it was Onesimus?

Chapter 11

nesimus was awakened by the smell of freshly baked bread. He had not been exposed to this aroma for such a long time that it made him especially hungry. As he opened his door to the hallway, Credo was just coming out of his room. "You were very exhilarated after leaving the assembly last night, then we noticed a quiet that came over you. Was something troubling you? We could not imagine that to be the case since you had just experienced the highlight of your life in being with Paul."

"Oh no, just tired, but anxious now to follow the aroma of the bread." Onesimus could not open up to anyone. He could not share the feelings he was having about the reluctance he had in answering any questions Paul may have of him.

When Onesimus and Credo went down to the table, Agus was already there. "Say Onesimus, are you still planning on going down to talk with Paul this morning? Surely by getting a special invitation such as that you will not let him down.

I understand when he gives a request such as that, he usually does not have anyone turn him down. I am thrilled for you in having this special invitation." Credo was encouraging Onesimus as much as he could.

"I wish that I could have been the one to have had the invitation to join Paul today. What an honor!" Agus put in his opinion realizing Onesimus was agonizing over something.

"If you don't remember the way, I will be happy to show you. Not that I have anything better to do this morning anyway," Credo spoke as he gave Onesimus a little push on his arm.

"I am still contemplating on whether I should go back or not. I tossed and turned most of the night realizing that a lot of what he said, as interesting as it was, was still way over my head. He used a lot of words that are unfamiliar to me and I am still trying to absorb most of it." Onesimus could see the disappointment on their faces.

"Tell you what, if Paul's talking gets to be too much for you, just tell him to slow down. But I will assure you, he will not tell you more than you can handle. He has a way about him that can see through people. I think the term some people use is 'discernment'. He will understand exactly where you are. He not only has a gift of edification but he can read people and know their hearts." Credo was still trying; he saw qualities in Onesimus that should not be wasted.

"All done with your meal I see. Come on Onesimus, Credo, let's head that way. I am sure Paul is up and about by now. It's like he said, he is not going anywhere." Agus was not giving up.

As they arrived at Paul's place, they gently knocked on the strong, wooden door and before long, a soldier opened the door, Paul greeted them right away with a hearty smile and strong hug. This morning he had chains attached around his ankles and soldiers very close by. The men were so saddened to see him this way.

"Oh, you have not disappointed me. I am so glad you came, Onesimus, You have brought your friends with you as well. You were also here last evening. I remember you being here now. Is that not correct?" Paul then gave them another big brotherly hug and invited them in to sit.

"My name is Agus and this is my brother in the Lord, Credo. We have sat under your teaching before. We always marvel at how you make the Scriptures come alive and we bask in each and every word. Together we daily read the passages from the Prophets and the writings of David. We cannot understand all they have to say to us, but you bring new insight to the reading. We met Onesimus on the ship that sailed in from Athens that docked here only yesterday. We worked together

and also shared many wonderful evenings reading the Word."
.Agus said wondering if he and Credo should stay.

"Onesimus, will you be able to find your way around if Credo and I go ahead and leave you two together? I believe you have things to discuss," Agus asked, and waited to see if Paul wanted to include them or if he had something in mind that was only for Onesimus.

Paul felt led to only be spending quality time with Onesimus so he answered the question for him "He will be fine. I assure you he will find his way home. Now you go along your way and enjoy the city. It has been my pleasure to make your acquaintance and I am appreciative of your taking Onesimus under your wing. Please do come back and we will share more time together."

After Credo and Agus left, Paul noticed that Onesimus appeared to be a little fidgety. "Well now, come on back and sit. Would you like a little refreshment on this warm day?"

"Oh, I am just fine. Please tell me all the places you have been. It seems you have traveled a lot and done so many things. Your life has been fuller than most anyone I know. Has the way been easy for you?" Onesimus was focusing on Paul to take attention off himself, hoping that Paul would overlook where he was from and not make connection with his past.

"There is plenty of time for that. Right now I want to hear if you know of any news from my friends in Colossae. I do not remember what you said your connection was to Epaphras? You realize he is the one who started the first church in Colossae. I spent three years in Ephesus and during that time, I met Epaphras. We became very close. He was an excellent student of the word and had such a gift, consequently, I laid hands on him and sent him off. It was no time until I heard that he had started a church in the home of a dear brother, Philemon." at the mention of that name, Paul noticed a little discomfort in Onesimus's manner.

"Philemon is a very genuine and generous man who immediately offered his home to the opening of God's Word to the community there in Colossae. He and Epaphras have a very close relationship. Maybe you know him." Paul noticed Onesimus was becoming quite pale and a little restless. He wondered if he had stumbled on a sensitive area.

"Onesimus, are you all right? Let me give you a drink. What seems to be the trouble?" Paul felt as though he had struck a sensitive nerve, but was uncertain what the problem was.

"I am fine. I am quite anxious to find out more about you. What shall I call you?" Onesimus knew he had to contain himself if he was going to accomplish anything here.

"Please call me Paul as everyone else does. I am just a man like everyone else and am humbled to have you as my guest today." Paul knew that he needed to get to the point, but did not want to scare this young man off. "But truly before we go further, I just have to know more about the area where you came from. Do you know if the church in Colossae is growing? Please forgive me for being too inquisitive, but my heart is on the new converts there. I need to know what news you would have for me."

Onesimus was hoping that Paul did not see him squirm as he was searching for answers to his questions. He had learned from the readings that he should not bear false witness, but would the truth be too high a price to pay? He had to think of something or else his hesitation would soon give him away for sure. "I was really a youth when I left there and I did not get out much." Onesimus was hoping that would be sufficient for Paul and he would not have to elaborate any further.

Paul was not reading anything into Onesimus's body language but was just generally curious. "You surely heard of Philemon. He is probably the wealthiest man in the area. He owns quite a lot of property and has a very nice family. I met Philemon on one of my journeys to Ephesus. He apparently goes there quite often to do some trading. He is a very, very kind-hearted man. And one for whom I have tremendous respect. I would certainly like to hear about him. Please tell me that you know of him so that I might be informed."

Before Onesimus could control what came out of his mouth, he was hearing himself say. "Yes, I know him and his wife. I know exactly where they live. Yes, he is very noble and gracious." Had he gone too far? Had he said too much? Maybe, just maybe, Paul would not pursue any further. Perchance that was all he wanted to know. Onesimus realized he could not volunteer much more information or he would be the one in chains.

"I get letters from Epaphras on occasion and it has not been too long since I received one. He did tell me that Philemon was a little disappointed in one thing. Let me think what it was that disturbed him so. Oh, yes one of his trusted slaves had run away. If I could find that letter, I would be able to know more about it. There has been so much happen to me. I cannot recall all the particulars. What I know and remember about Philemon, he would be a very gracious and kind man to work for. From what I understand, he does not treat his slaves harshly, more like what we would consider servants." Paul seemed disappointed in knowing that his brother in the Lord had to go through the grief of this loss.

Onesimus had to come up with something really quick. "I understand that Philemon is a very good man and treats his slaves kindly. I guess the person who ran away had just had enough and wanted to explore the rest of the world. Even though he was good to his slaves, it was not like …, I mean it was not like his slaves could come and go as they pleased. You know it is really difficult having no freedom and seeing others pursue life as they please and not be able to. Oh I am sorry, please forgive me. Talking to you like this, I forgot you are also in that same kind of position right now."

"You must understand, Onesimus, that I count it an honor to be in chains for my Lord. Do not feel sorry for me. However, you sound almost as if you are talking firsthand about being in bondage. Do you know of someone close to you who has experienced a similar situation?" Paul just realized he may be getting a little too close to home for Onesimus.

"Oh yes, I have known some slaves. I understand that most of them are content especially living under Philemon, but they do not know any other kind of life. They have never left the property and seen a better way of life. They are so tied down to what they have always had that leaving it would be too hard to do. There is a better way out there and it is called freedom." Onesimus had no doubt he had gone too far in his rampage, but all the things he had just said were patterned after his own life.

"You know, dear child, what you are describing is life with Christ and life without Him. This is a good illustration of what I most often speak about. He is also that better life, and those who have never experienced Him do not realize what they are missing. They are the ones who are really living in bondage. There is a better life in Him to be lived out to the fullest. Those who live in the world and have never tasted the joy and peace in knowing Him, then they are the ones who are truly tied down to the life they have always lived out of ignorance. And talk about freedom. True freedom comes in a life lived in serving Jesus Christ the Lord as your personal Savior." Paul knew he needed to share his insights with this eager learner of the Word.

"Please, if you do not mind, would you teach me about this Savior? You are the first one to ever tell me about that and you also mentioned something last night about the Holy Spirit? That is a term I have never heard before and you seem to be very sold on it and you want others to know about it as well. I would like the opportunity to hear more. Are you willing to do this one-on-one for a little while?" Onesimus was wanting to change the subject from Philemon while also eager to find out what Paul was talking about.

Before they knew it, a guard was bringing in plates of food that had been dropped off and there was plenty for the two of them. Onesimus was very pleased that he was included in this for he was experiencing hunger pangs. The day went on and no more mention was made of Onesimus's past life, and for that he was delighted. It was a glorious day and lots of new information had been stored in his mind that would not soon be forgotten.

"You are a very good student, Onesimus. I take pride in your attention to the Scriptures. It is so hard to believe that you have never come in contact with the gospel until just very recently. I will be very disappointed if you do not come back tomorrow." Paul was delighted to be able to tutor a young scholar with such potential and eagerness to learn.

"If that is an invitation, then I accept. You will see me here at the same time. Have a good night's rest." Onesimus left mentally drained, but rejoiced in his new adventure.

When Agus heard Onesimus coming up the steps heading toward his door, he stuck his head out of his room very curious as to where Onesimus had been all the day. "Credo and I were so concerned about you. It has been a big part of the day since we left you at Paul's house. Where have you been, may I ask? Did you get lost in this large city? Are you all right? Did you find something to eat? Please fill me in as we are quite interested in your safety and well-being." Agus was genuinely anxious to get all the details.

"You will never believe it, just as I am having trouble believing it myself, but I have been at the home of Paul ever since you left me there this morning. We have just been sharing and studying the Scriptures all day. My mind is overwhelmed with so much new knowledge that I can hardly contain myself. He is so well-versed in God's written Word. I consider myself very honored to sit at his feet and have Scripture made so clear to me. I am finding that God is a good God and he has a plan for my life. Paul just wants me to be sure and know God personally and know God has a future for me. ME! I feel so special. I cannot believe I am saying that because I am so unworthy." Onesimus remembered his upbringing and realized he had just been existing, but at this point felt he was actually worthy.

"Let me awaken Credo. He is going to want to hear all about this. He is probably not asleep anyway since we were so fearful for your well-being," Agus said as he knocked on Credo's door.

"I was not asleep, just dozing a little. Onesimus, please explain to me all that has happened with you today. I am just so thankful that you are safe." Credo was relieved to know that Onesimus was there with them, noticing the peace that he was displaying.

"Please come into my room and I will begin to explain a little of my time with Paul. First of all, there is not one moment of the day that those guards do not have their eye on him, and sometimes, they come right over and attach themselves to him with those horrible iron cuffs. He takes it all in stride, though, I must say that about him. Now getting down to what you really want to hear about how my day has gone. It is so amazing that I knew nothing of God much less His Word until you two started reading to me just a few weeks ago. Now I realize that God has chosen me and He has a plan for my life. The more I hear, the more I want to know about what God has to say in these parchments," he said as he pointed to the tablet that Credo brought with him. "How can I ever thank you enough for introducing me to Paul and even bringing me to the place where I am now? Paul just read to me all day. He would take the Prophets' words and explain their meaning showing me that so much of those passages have just been fulfilled by One dying on the cross. I am appalled at how much he knows and how he gets this information." Onesimus knew he would never be able to tell these two dear men what all happened during the course of the day.

Credo was wide awake now and wanted Onesimus to be sure and know how glad he was for him. "Please know the pleasure is all ours. We were happy to open the Word to you. We are even more pleased that you have had the opportunity to sit at the feet of the master teacher. Tell me, will you go to Paul's home again? Did he give you an invitation to return?"

Agus knew as soon as Credo asked the question, what the answer was from the expression on Onesimus's face. "Yes, I am delighted to say I will be returning early tomorrow. I will not be staying very long because the guards are going to limit my time there. Apparently it was unusual that they allowed me to be there for the entire time today. I think they were really annoyed at hearing the word 'God' and 'Lord' so much."

Chapter 12

fter two more days of instruction, Onesimus knew that he would prefer staying in Rome instead of returning to Athens on the ship. He was not looking forward to being with those brutish men again that he would have to work with day in and day out. Also, what would going back there have to offer him? Onesimus realized he made enough money on that trip so he could afford to live here for a while. Surely he would be able to get a job around Rome. He would be certain to get some sound advice from Paul.

"Good day, my son." Paul greeted Onesimus at his front door in the usual manner with the chains attached to his ankles but as usual in a very uplifted manner. "How are you doing on such a lovely day?"

"It is always a very good day when I can see you, Paul. I hope you are doing well, also," Onesimus replied with an extra glimmer in his eye. "You seem especially joyous this morning. Has anything changed with you?"

"You are very perceptive, I must say. As a matter of fact I have just received news that my dear friend and son in the faith, Timothy, will be paying me a visit quite soon. It always does my heart good to see him. It saddens me though, that you may not be around when he comes since, I believe, your ship sails back to Athens in a very few days."

"That is what I want to talk to you about. You see, I have been thinking very seriously of not returning back when the ship leaves on Thursday. I would like to stay in Rome in view of the fact that I have way more going for me here than I could possibly think would come my way if I left. I am waiting to hear if you will support my decision." Onesimus realized that maybe he was being somewhat forward since he had only known Paul for such a short time.

"Why, child, I think that is an excellent idea. Are you sure you have thought it through carefully, though? It is a big decision for you to make on an impulse, you know." Paul was elated but wanted to be sure Onesimus was staying for all the right reasons.

"I am glad you approve. May I continue to be a part of your life? I would love to hear more about Timothy and hope that you are willing to tell me all about him, so that if we do visit together, I will be enlightened. I realize that I will have to get a job because I will be giving up my pay that I was making on the ship, but there is most likely something I can do and still have time to visit with you. Your influence is the main reason I want to stay and that would allow me not to be with the scum that I would otherwise have to work with on the ship back to Athens." Onesimus could not believe he had just said that.

"Onesimus, you must not judge others so harshly. We are all God's children and those men have not had the opportunities that you have. I, of all people, know what it is like to be persecuted, but we must love those who persecute us as well as those who love us in return. I am so glad you enjoy my company, and I yours. We will see what we can work out by your remaining behind." Paul began to think things through in hopes that an opening for Onesimus would come around.

"I can keep my room as long as I am able to pay for it. I do have some money set aside, so I will be financially sound for a while. Credo and Agus want to show me around the city tomorrow. They would like me to be involved in some of the things Rome has to offer while we have the opportunity to be together. So I will not be here tomorrow. I do not want you to worry if I do not show up." Onesimus could tell from Paul's expression that he totally approved.

"You go and have a good time with your young friends tomorrow. They are good people and I trust them with you wholeheartedly. Please have them come before they depart so that I might wish them well on their journey back to Athens." Paul used the time with Onesimus this particular day to share more deeply his own conversion experience and also worked on teaching him to do a portion of the reading from God's Word. He pointed out such words as "blessed, Shepherd, love, Lord, trust, soul, and sacrifice." he wanted this young man to be able to pick up God's Word and be able to enjoy it on his own. After this session, he wished him well until they meet again the day after his 'day on the town'.

Onesimus realized that the drawback to his decision would be in missing the companionship of his new friends. How would he ever be able to let them know what he had decided? Just as he was mulling that over in his mind, a peace came over him that assured him they would understand.

Now he would have to think about how to handle letting the people who were in charge of the ship know that he would not be going back with them and that they would have to seek a replacement. He thought that the sooner he did it, the better it would be. He had never resigned from a position prior to this, and he was not sure of the appropriate way to handle it. "The best thing for me to do is go ahead and inform Credo and Agus and they will then help me with the other matter," Onesimus reasoned with himself.

"Credo, Agus there you are. I have been looking for you." Onesimus found the men right around the corner from where they were staying just sitting at a little table enjoying a cool drink. "I need to speak with you about a decision that I have made."

"This sounds really serious, Onesimus, please tell us. We are interested in knowing what has gotten you so keyed up." Agus wondered what was on his mind.

"I am very reluctant to tell you what I have decided and I hope you understand the significance of my decision. I have a change of plans." Before Onesimus could finish, Credo interrupted. "Let me finish for you. You are making plans to stay here in Rome where you feel you are being led."

"Well, yes, that is correct, but how did you know when I have just made the decision myself?" Onesimus was taken by surprise.

With a laugh that could have been heard all the way to the coliseum, Credo answered. "There has been nothing more apparent in all the world than the growing relationship you have had with Paul and the connection the two of you have made in such a short period of time. You go to see him early each morning and return late in the day and all you talk about when you are with us, only in the evenings I might add, is Paul this and Paul that. Oh, and of course, you do share with us a good deal of what he has taught you during the day. Onesimus, you would be lost without Paul in your life right now."

"I am so very sorry that I have neglected the two of you. I did not realize that I had been gone from you that much. I guess that when I am with him, the time just goes by so quickly, and I did not realize how much time I have actually spent with him." Onesimus was quite embarrassed as he apologized to the two of them.

"Of course, we do understand. Think nothing of having neglected us. That really has not been a problem for us. We do enjoy your company and have valued your friendship and our time spent together, but your priority has been in the time spent with Paul. He has been very good for you." Agus made it clear to Onesimus that their feelings were not the issue here at all.

"That brings me to another issue that I am not looking forward to, and I covet your helping me in this matter."

"Let us think what we could possibly do that might be of assistance to you in any way. We have introduced you to some very fine Christian men who would do anything for you, found a very lovely room for you to sleep in at night, shown you around some of the best areas of Rome, and taken you to some fine eating establishments. What more could we do to help you?" Credo asked this with a sheepish grin on his face as if he already knew the answer to his question.

"I know this is asking a lot, but could the two of you please come with me to the pier first thing in the morning? Since I have made my decision to remain here, I cannot think of how I should approach the men on the ship to inform them what my plans are. I have never left a job before and I really do not know how to go about it. My stomach is in knots just thinking about talking with that big fellow. All the positions I have left have been as a promotion that the owners have worked out themselves for my betterment." No one could possibly resist Onesimus's plea.

"We will go with you for moral support; however, that only gives them two days to find your replacement. Not to minimize your duties or to make you feel as though you can easily be replaced, but it will not take them long to find a new employee to do your job." Agus did not want to hurt his feelings, but he also wanted him to be sure and know that it would not be a hardship on the crew.

"Well, thanks a lot," Onesimus teased with them, "I know I am not indispensable but you could boost me up just a little."

"No, really, there are always strong, willing men just ready for positions to open up. Good-paying jobs are hard to come by and the men here are usually ready to sail the big seas for a new adventure. So do not feel bad at all in going to them tomorrow and letting them know you are staying here in Rome. That happens a lot. But if you would trust my opinion, there is something I feel you should know." Agus suddenly looked very serious.

"Yes, please. I would gladly heed any advice you might have." Onesimus was looking a little worried at this point.

Agus cleared his throat and was very careful in how he would word what he felt he needed to say, "You are well aware of the fact that these seamen are not Christians. So if you told them that you are staying back to study Scriptures, or even that Paul is in the process of teaching you and you want to continue that, then they would laugh you off of the entire coastline. I am just saying that you do not have to give them a reason for your staying. It is really none of their business why you will not be returning."

Onesimus looked a little confused, "I was not sure what I was going to give them for an excuse as to why I would not be joining them on the return trip, but I am not embarrassed to let them know why. I am very proud of what I have accomplished over the last few days, and I do not mind sharing that information with anyone. However, if you feel I should not let them know that, then I will respect your opinion. Credo, do you feel the same as Agus?"

"I most certainly do. To you it seems no harm in explaining your reasoning, but in the long run it could be detrimental to the Cause. These robust sailors meet up with a lot of influential people all over the world, as we know it. If they thought this was a laughing matter to be shared, then we do not want you, or especially not Paul to be the bad end of their jokes. So some things are better left not said." Agus also gave his opinion.

"All right, if you both agree. I just take great pride in the Gospel, and I feel everyone should have exposure to it, especially since those people are the kind of people who really need to know. I guess I understand what you are saying, even though I do not approve. I will not volunteer my reasons for staying, and if I am asked to explain, I will just be prepared to give them no reason at all." Onesimus agreed this would not be so difficult after all in resigning his position.

"How about if we go down to the pier first thing tomorrow and then take the day to tour the city and have a really good time together? This will give us our last full day together." Credo was just inspired to celebrate.

"Yes, let us show Onesimus some of the culture here and what the men do for entertainment. I imagine we can introduce him to things he never thought existed." Agus added to Credo's thoughts

As the three men approached the pier and went straight to the ship that would take them back to Athens, they noticed a really long line of men eager to seek employment. At that point Onesimus knew his speaking with his superior would be softened.

"That was not so bad," Onesimus said to his friends. "They did not even flinch when I told them that I preferred staying on here and they accepted my resignation quite well. I did not even feel the urge to explain that I would be doing errands and helping Paul out. You know, now that I think of it, I realize that I will again be a servant, but this time with a willing heart and I will be doing it with a person I have quickly come to love."

"See, we told you that they get used to the resignations and it happens more than you think. They usually have strong men who can pull their weight on handling the boat just ready for a position to open. The availability is always there. Plenty of people are anxious to sail the wide seas so they are prepared for this to happen. Quite often people such as yourself get to the big city of Rome and want to stay around for a while." Credo was quick to encourage him.

"I truly want to thank the two of you for coming with me. You made this task much easier." Onesimus wanted to be sure they knew how much he appreciated their backing him up.

As they were walking away from the pier, Agus made the statement "We sure are going to miss having you along on our trip back. If it was not for family back home, I would be so tempted to stay with you. You were the first ray of sunshine we have had for a very long time. The trip will not be nearly as interesting; however, as we continue our readings each night but be assured that we will think about God's provision in your life."

"I have never seen anything so enormous. Again, tell me what you call it?" Onesimus could not help but contain his excitement as he viewed the inside of the large open building. "There is so much stone all over the place. It must have taken forever to mix this all up, pour it out, and form the ramps and flooring."

"This is the Coliseum. Let us take a seat and you will be very surprised as what we are going to watch. But keep in mind that this is the most favorite form of entertainment this city has to offer. Whenever the men have a chance to come, they do so. There have been times when we have been here that this whole place has been full and men are standing around all over." Agus was delighted to explain to him.

"The lions are released from underneath,." Agus went on to explain, "and we are in a very good position to be able to see the people who are working the machines that pull the animal cages and allow the lions to charge at the gladiators."

It did not take Onesimus long to realize that the men below who were trudging around the heavy stone were slaves. Their lives were not their own. How well Onesimus understood their lot in life. If only he could go to them and tell them the freedom they could have in their hearts by accepting Jesus. Even though they would still have to be loyal to their masters, they could still have free souls.

All Onesimus could think to say was "Those poor men. I really feel sorry for them having to give all their strength to push that heavy piece of wood around just for the pleasure of everyone else. I wish with all my heart that I could go down there and release them. Life is so unfair to them."

"Why Onesimus, I did not know you felt so strongly about such matters and have a soft and compassionate heart. I, too, wish that they were not in this great bondage, but I really never gave it much thought. There really is no other way, if we are to enjoy the competition. I just felt it was part of the act and did not consider their feelings." Credo felt guilty that he had never regarded anything but the pleasure he was having in enjoying the show.

"Let us just have a good time and not let our minds get absorbed in the issues that we can do nothing about. Look, there is another lion being released. Where but Rome could you enjoy such a spectacle?" Agus always looked forward to the entertainment whenever he had the opportunity.

Onesimus settled back and viewed the huge arena, and was in awe of all the magnificent architecture. He lost himself in the excitement all around him.

When they left, they had worked up an appetite but did not take long to come across an open baker's shop that was known for its round loaves of the most delicious bread in the city. They walked on to find a market of some kind of fish Onesimus had never had and it was most delicious. Onesimus was amazed at all the children who were coming back from school. Only groups of boys, though, as he understood the girls were taught at home. That is not unusual since he had been aware of that while he was living in Miletus. What was most impressive to Onesimus as he toured the city was the way the women dressed. He noticed the ornate jewelry they wore. He could tell they were very fond of their jewelry. The women also had extremely unusual looking hair, so much so that he had trouble believing it was natural.

"I have never seen women have such strange-colored hair before. Is this something that is normal for women of Rome? Why have I not seen these colors before?" Onesimus asked very seriously.

Agus replied, "That was strange for me to understand the first time I was here. The women of wealth have so much time on their hands since they do not have to do domestic duties that they get very bored. One of the things to occupy themselves is to have their hair dyed and the more unusual the color, the better. They sometimes powder it with gold dust or add false blond hair that is imported from Germanic tribes. They do come up with some of the strangest colors, do they not?"

"That is just so peculiar to me that someone would want to do that. I just have such a hard time with people who have so much leisure time and more money than they know what to do with, and on the other hand there are the people who do not have any time or money for themselves." Onesimus must have sounded harsh in his response.

"Why Onesimus, you are becoming a really deep thinker. I can see your point, but there again, I guess I have not given it much thought," Agus replied, quite surprised in Onesimus's attitude.

"I have also never seen so much jewelry in my life. That lady we just passed was wearing more gold than I have ever seen. Do they think it makes them more beautiful to wear it? Tell me, what is the purpose?" Onesimus was really curious as to why the women in this area got so dressed up.

"I suppose that is their custom. Their husbands have powerful positions, and it is important to them for their wives to be beautiful. I guess that helps them to be 'somebody' when their wives look fashionable. Everyone looks at them and thinks their husbands must be successful." Agus tried to explain what was customary in this region.

"We have more things to show you, let us go ahead and look around. We still have a lot of territory to cover." Credo wanted the day to be memorable and not be a downer for them.

"Thank you so much for the wonderful day and for showing me around this huge city. I could have never ventured out on my own like we did today. It has meant so much to me to be able to have had this time together. I will not be looking forward to our goodbyes tomorrow." Onesimus shared his feelings with the two friends.

"We feel the same way. We have deeply enjoyed our time with you. This was a great day. You made it very nice for us. You have opened our eyes to areas we needed to think upon. Thank you for making us aware of issues we need to be considerate of." Agus spoke with conviction as he reflected on the equality or lack of it of a man's status in life.

"I must say that I am a little apprehensive with our parting company. I have learned to depend on you for so many things and it will be very different with you leaving." Onesimus said to Credo and Agus as they said their good-byes at the pier.

"You are truly our brother now. We take pride in the way you have grown so very much in the short time we have been together. We have also learned to depend on you. You have given us such great comfort and companionship," Credo said with tears in his eyes, not knowing what was ahead for his new brother, but realizing that his future was in God's hands.

As Agus gave Onesimus a hug and kiss on the cheek he also, with tears in his eyes said, "No greater love have I had for any man than I have had for you. I do not know much about your past, and you realize that has not been important to me. Just know that I am interested in your future, and I know it will be a bright one for you."

As Credo also gave Onesimus a kiss on the cheek accompanied by a big hug, he imparted a solemn good-bye wondering if their paths would ever cross again, "Please know that I will be praying for you and trusting you are in God's care. I will miss you, but you will be entrusted to Paul's guidance and he will not let you down. Be safe and continue on with the readings. Next time we see you, we will be sitting at your feet with you explaining the Scriptures to us because you will know far more than we do. If you are ever in Delphi, please look us up. Take care brother, and God bless."

Onesimus stayed at the pier and waved good-bye to them as the ship became a tiny vessel on the mighty seas, and hoping in his heart that he would one day meet up again with these precious newfound brothers in the Lord.

Chapter 13

As Onesimus entered the door of Paul's rented house, his heart was deeply saddened when he heard the clang, clang, clang of the chains around Paul's ankles as he shuffled to the entrance to meet his guest. He had become accustomed to this sound for quite some time now; however, today he was especially sensitive to the sound. All he could think of at that moment was the fact that this was truly a man of God and why did he have to suffer so? He could be out ministering to others. He could be resuming his travels to far-off lands as he so often spoke of having done in the past. "Why, why, why," Onesimus wondered, "did the God of great power and love have to leave Paul, his trusted servant, in such a state?"

"Good morning, my dear young man! Why the sad face? It could not be the weather but I notice how lovely and bright the sun shines today. Please share with me what is troubling you." Paul thought he knew but he wanted to hear Onesimus express himself, to really show his feelings as he has just begun to open up to him. When Paul first met him, Onesimus was very passive and always seemed frightened to show what was going on inside of himself.

"I am so saddened to see you, my mentor, in chains and tied up here like an animal. I hate it that I am free and able to walk the streets when I don't deserve to do so and there you are, one who has done nothing wrong to anyone, being kept here under arrest, and you have LOST your freedom. I know a little of what you are going through." Onesimus could not believe he was explaining this to Paul, but Paul trusted him and before this relationship went any further, he had to get some things out in the open.

"Child, do not feel guilty that you are free to go your way with no restrictions. That is life. I got caught in the act of speaking forth in the name of Jesus Christ and caused contempt to the officials. I was asked time and again to neglect this crusade, but I chose not to abandon the cause. I would rather forfeit my own life than cease to speak the truth of the resurrection power of my Lord and Savior. Enjoy the liberation you have that has been given to you so freely." Paul sincerely spoke to Onesimus.

"I know all that. But I really do not understand and probably never will. If I feel guilty, it is not about that… not really." Onesimus was building up his courage.

"There is something else that is troubling you. I can sense there are things you are keeping from me. Maybe I can help if you will only allow me." Paul showed compassion in a way that Onesimus had never before seen.

"How am I possibly going to find the words to tell you what my heart has been aching to say for so long now. I am afraid I will be taking a chance of risking the relationship that we share, and I cannot bear to lose you. You see I do not have the most innocent past. Please find it in your heart to forgive me of what I must confess to you." Onesimus's heart was pounding but he knew he needed to be honest to this faithful follower of the Truth.

Paul observed the reluctance in his manner, he needed to hear what Onesimus had to say. "Please continue, my son. Do not be fearful. There is nothing you could have possibly done that would keep me from forgiving you."

Paul took a hold of Onesimus's hands, which were cold and clammy.

"Onesimus, dear, precious, child, why do you tremble so? What could have possibly happened that has put such a fright in you? Whatever it is, we can certainly work it out. There is nothing you could have ever done that would make me turn from you. You must believe me." Paul was genuinely concerned for his son in the Lord.

"I hope you still feel the same after I share my past with you. As you know, I am from Colossae and I was not born a free person. My father and mother are still confined to the life I should be living now. I was owned by other people and trapped forever; therefore, I begrudged every day I had to get up and work for them. Taking orders, working hard, and not having a life of my own was how it was destined to be forever. I felt trapped. So one day, I had enough and I chose to leave. The term is runaway. Yes, sir, I am a runaway slave. Like I said, my past is not a pretty one, but choosing to escape was not the honest thing to do." It was now out in the open. Paul was the only one who knew what hideous thing he had done. How was Paul going to handle it? Was he going to find out who Onesimus's master was and turn him in? That would be the only thing he could do, especially being friends with Philemon. He would surely have an "F" branded on his forehead now and be sent back to lead a more horrible life than what he had before. Everyone then would know he was a fugitive. He realized he had befriended Paul, but how much allegiance could he expect from him?

"Why do you not look surprised? Please say something now that I have poured out my life to you." Onesimus was puzzled at Paul's lack of expression.

"My heart breaks for you, my dear child. I have felt all along that there was something deep inside of you that needed to come out so you could become more wholesome. You know, until you own up to your trespasses, you can never claim the victory you so want to have in your heart. Please continue. I am listening and will not judge you. I am only here to help and try to guide you." Paul was very understanding as Onesimus poured out his soul to him.

Onesimus hesitated in going further. He thought he had said all that he really needed to and was feeling very uncomfortable even to his mentor and close friend. Although Paul appeared to be sympathetic and understanding, the rest was very hard for Onesimus to share.

Paul sensed how much suffering Onesimus was going through so he decided to help him along. "Onesimus, my dear son, could it be that the one from whom you ran away was my brother Philemon? I believe it is all coming together now. Remember the letter I told you about? After you appeared quite uncomfortable at the mention of it, I hunted it up and put the pieces together. At that point, I had not gotten to really know you and was not sure of your capabilities, but now I am proud to say, I do know what a good, solid person you really are. I tried not to believe this same person that betrayed Philemon could be you, but it seems as though my fears have come true. It is not that I am being deceptive, but I was waiting for the appropriate time that we would be able to get this secret out in the open. I know you are a good person, Onesimus. I also know how a young heart reacts, after all, freedom and being out on your own were very important to you. You saw the life your father and mother and their fathers and mothers before them lived and you did not want to live that way. You were eager to make it better for yourself and in view of that, you seized an opportunity." Paul was relieved they had exposed the secret that they both were keeping— Paul in actually knowing the truth and Onesimus afraid to admit that he was a runaway.

"You have known for this long, or at least suspected the information you received from Philemon was about me? I feel so torn. A part of me feels as though you were watching me very closely to see if I would betray you and the other part of me cannot believe you had it in your heart to still take me under your wing in total trust. I do not think I could have been as kind as you." Onesimus breathed a sigh of relief. "I actually should have been open with you before the ship left for Athens, just in case you were not receptive and I still had a chance for my old job."

"Let me explain a little further." Paul said. "As tired as I was that evening that we met, I was determined to find Philemon's letter. I finally located it and was actually trembling as I read it. I mentioned to you then that I remembered he told me of the runaway slave that so saddened him. I knew he included the name of the slave, but I could not remember what that name was. My heart skipped a beat or two when I came to the name. It was yours, Onesimus. I, also, was full of grief. Sorrow overtook me when I came to know I was in the presence of the one who had made my dear friend in Christ so sad. I put it upon myself to not say anything in view of the fact that I saw great potential in you, Onesimus." Paul saw that Onesimus was looking more relaxed. They both knew they could move on now with no hidden secrets.

Paul continued, "Right from the beginning I knew you had a lot to give. You were genuinely eager to learn from the Word and I could not turn my back on that. I long to draw closer to you even now so let us continue to work together and when the time comes, we will do what we need to do. But until then, we will be led by the direction of the Holy Spirit. I am not finished with you yet; the Lord is still working on you, and you are not ready to conclude the earnest desires of your heart which is revelation of the Scriptures."

Onesimus needed to have some questions answered and asked Paul, "So how much time do you give me? How long will it be before you let Philemon in on our secret? Am I going to feel secure in staying here, or should I be threatened from day to day that my time is up? Please feel confident in the fact that I am not planning on running away from here because I do not think I could handle being on the run again. That was a very terrifying time for me, but actually, being under Philemon was not all that bad as I look back. The treatment

I had to endure working on the big boat coming over here far outweighed any cruelty I could have ever imagined while living in Colossae. He was a very kind master and even though I never really knew him personally, my father did and he had a lot of respect for that man. I now appreciate his position." Onesimus realized he was rambling due to the anxiety he suddenly felt.

"I must warn you that under Roman law, the slave is not considered a man, but a chattel without any civil rights whatever, completely at the mercy of his master. There is no law to interfere on behalf of the slave no matter how cruel the master is to him. We must never let any of the authorities here in Rome have the remotest idea that you are a runaway slave. In their eyes you would still be considered a slave and I would not like to think of the consequences. There is no reason for anyone to suspect that you are anything other than my companion. You will be safe as long as we keep it our secret and possibly only a select few would I trust with this information." Paul did not want to speculate what might happen to Onesimus if this news got in the wrong hands.

"What is so wonderful about God's grace," Paul resumed, "is that all people in the church are a brotherhood. In Christ Jesus there is neither bond nor free, male or female. All stand on a footing of equality before the Lord; all are brethren, all

God's children and are bound to each other by the ties of brotherly love."

"I am so thankful that I am a part of that kind of family. I do trust you and respect whatever measure you feel we need to take." Onesimus was thankful Paul did not take his responsibilities lightly.

"To add to that" Paul wanted to clarify for Onesimus, "The servant is to continue to render faithful service to the master who is a beloved brother, and the master is to love and trust his servant as a brother."

"You have my respect and trust. It is no wonder that people pack the room to see you. God gave you so many gifts and wisdom is at the top." Onesimus realized how thankful he was to be a part of this great man's life.

"You can rest assured that I am not going to turn on you. Like I said I am not finished with you yet. We still have a ways to go. Actually, I am also being selfish. You have so far been a great asset to me, and I need you here with me to continue on in my ministry as you have so earnestly been doing since you decided to stay in Rome As you can fully see, I am very limited in what I can do and being confined to this house, I am not able to provide for my own needs. I am comfortably set financially due to the fact that so many churches that I had visited over the years are supplying my needs. I was never comfortable with that when I was physically able to work for myself; however, I now graciously accept financial help in order to continue what I was called to do." Indeed, Onesimus, I truly need your help," Paul added, quite enthused in hoping Onesimus might continue to serve him while he was under house arrest.

Onesimus indeed brightened up "Help you? I would be very privileged to continue to assist you in anything I can. You know that, so please do not hesitate telling me what you need to have done and I will do what I have been doing and much more."

"Yes, I know that." Paul was quite pleased with the way things were working out. "This is one of the blessings of God in that He is always there to supply our every need. As a matter of fact, I am about out of parchment–papyrus and, oh yes, some oil also that I use for making the ink. There is a place where these can be purchased about three streets from here. While I am thinking of supplies, there is a certain salve I need to keep me comfortable. You see I have a problem around my eyes which dates back to when I was blinded for three days. Did I ever tell you that story? Oh, of course I did no doubt six or seven times. My conversion experience was something else and one I will never forget; anyway, it is important for me to use this salve which is so very soothing. Would you be kind enough to now go after those items for me? I am very behind on my correspondence and will need those things to resume."

"I am on my way. May I suggest that we have a celebration together now that my burdens have been lifted? The store across the street and around the corner has a special on mutton that they already have prepared and pomegranate sounds delicious to me as well. How do you feel about sharing in a little feast?" An excited Onesimus left and Paul could not help but notice him kicking up his heels and feeling a new kind of freedom that he had never felt before. "If only Onesimus knew these supplies will be used to write letters to the church at Colassae on his behalf," Paul said to himself.

Paul knew that a weight had been lifted from Onesimus. He had not realized until now what kind of bondage Onesimus had really been under. Now that he had released his inward burdens, he could be free to really serve Christ in a new way.

Onesimus spoke to himself with a grin clear across his face "Now I have the opportunity to really help a father figure and trusted companion in the Lord."

Chapter 14

Paul was so glad that he decided to nurture Onesimus along, even though if he were discovered doing so, his own life could be in even more danger,. "I believe he will prove to be very valuable to me in fellowship as well as be my hands and feet while I am restrained here. I spent many days wondering how I would ever accomplish the things I needed to do. Now this dear boy is able to do all my running and deliver messages to my fellow workers. He has such drive. He reminds me of myself when I was much younger and he has a portion of Timothy in him as well. I all too well know the law, and it requires that he be returned to his original master. I can only trust that he will not be found out any time soon. If I did not turn him over to his master, then I would be expected to release him to the authorities. I do know that I could not live with myself if I did that, and I would feel as though I had betrayed him. Only the Lord knows what would happen to him then. Subsequently, he could even be sold by them and I would never hear from him again. No, I could not release him to the officials, for he would definitely be treated very harshly. He, like Timothy, is my spiritual son, a brand new believer and my trusted friend." Paul knew silence in this case was a virtue.

"Good morning, Onesimus, did you rest well last evening? It is always a pleasure to see you." Paul knew he had to nurture him along more rapidly because he did not know how much longer he should harbor him.

"Yes, I rested very well and good morning to you. I trust you slept well since indeed you look very radiant today. Is there something special on your mind?" Onesimus knew that Paul had inner peace, but today he looked especially full of joy.

"I just got up this morning to the birds singing and the sun shining and I felt very privileged to be alive." Paul did feel quite happy today.

"You know I felt the same way also. Another day God has given me to be here, to serve you and journey through the fine streets of Rome as I seek to do your will." Onesimus felt as though he had finally mastered his way around town.

"There is something I need to discuss with you. I want you to be clear in knowing that what has happened to me has really served to advance the gospel. As a result of my being in chains, it has become clear throughout the whole palace guard that I am in bondage for Christ. Because of my situation, there is a deep compassion from the new believers; therefore, the things that I say have a deeper impact. They see how complacent and patient I am and they know it is only through the grace of God that I have this firm foundation that is contagious to the followers. Because of my chains, most of the brothers in the Lord have been encouraged to speak the word of God more courageously and fearlessly." Paul knew he had to speak with Onesimus openly and wanted to be sure he completely understood that God had been the one to place him where he was for a reason.

"I realize that because of your imprisonment, so many people have had the opportunity to benefit from your ministry who would not have otherwise been able. Even the guards who are constantly by your side surely benefit from hearing your messages. But you would still be better off walking the streets and enjoying your freedom." Onesimus understood what he was saying, but was a little confused at this reasoning.

"I know that what has happened to me, my being in chains and all, will turn out for my everlasting deliverance. I try to always have the mind and attitude of Christ Jesus and draw comfort from His love and fellowship with the Spirit. I want to stress to you, Onesimus, to do nothing out of selfish gain or vain conceit. Always think of Jesus first, others second, then yourself." Paul was trying to think of areas he had not specifically gone over with him.

"I am indeed working on that, sir," Onesimus said while he was emptying out the bag of supplies he had purchased.

They were then startled by a loud knock on the door and as a new guest came through, Paul was very happy to receive him. "Timothy, my son, I have been so anxious for you to meet my new friend. This is Onesimus who has been spending time with me and together, we have become partners in the gospel."

Timothy received Onesimus with joy as introductions were made. "Onesimus has been beneficial to this 'old man in prison'. I trust you will accept him in brotherly love just as I have done after we fill you in on his life story."

Timothy, of course, accepted Onesimus with grace and love and knew that if he was acceptable to Paul, then he would receive him with brotherly love as well.

Timothy then brought Paul up-to-date on 'the Cause', for which Timothy had been preaching on Paul's behalf. "Please accept my apologies for not having been here sooner, but I go where it is beneficial at the time. I have brought you some food that I think will last for a few days. I still have a hard time understanding why the Romans do not feed their prisoners. You have me and some of the other followers, but there are so many people who are locked up who do not have anyone."

"I trust you have time to join us in a meal, Timothy." and Paul was relieved when he accepted.

After the breaking of bread together, Timothy took off for a mission he had been given and hoped to return soon.

"So tell me. Is there any part of the Scripture that you would like us to expound on? Possibly something you remember when Credo and Agus read to you that you have any questions about?" Paul wanted to be sure to give Onesimus spiritual strength.

"We did not elaborate too much on the Commandments that Moses received. I suppose those were pretty clear. However, I would like you to explain them more if you would." Onesimus was testing Paul to see how he would identify with each of them.

Paul was a little surprised at his choice, "That is an excellent place in the Scripture to study today. I am a little taken aback that you would bring that portion up though. I assume we did not go into a great deal of detail, did we?"

As they went through each of the commandments, expounding on the first four that pertain to honoring God Himself, he then went on to the others and Paul found himself actually enjoying the teaching of these commands. He had not done a study on these for quite some time. From an early age, children are taught the Mosaic Laws and of all areas of the Scripture, that would be what would be known more than anything. For that reason, Paul usually went right to the Gospel of Jesus Christ.

When they came to the eighth commandment, 'Thou shalt not steal,' Paul explained, "When you steal from someone, you totally have lost their trust and if that happens it is hard to ever be accepted by them again. If we steal from a person, how can we love them? As was quoted by Moses, 'You must have honest and accurate weights and measures so that you may live long in the land the Lord your God has given you.' In other words, we need to be honest with all men and not do anything to be deceptive. This is perhaps one of the easiest of the commands to keep, if you think about it. What do you think, my son?" Paul knew he had not put any more emphasis on this particular commandment than he had any of the others, but he could not help but notice the anguish in Onesimus's face.

"I am sorry, so sorry. My heart aches just now because I am such a sinner. What should I do? I do not want anyone to not trust me, hence, I want very much to live an honest and whole life in the Lord. Paul, sir, I am a sinner. Please help me make it right." Onesimus was at this point crying profusely with his head down in his hands.

"My precious Onesimus, I do not understand. Please, please, whatever the problem is, it could not be so bad. Allow me to know what this burden is. You know I will try my best to help you, so please be open with me, son." Paul's heart was aching for his brother.

"I have sinned very badly. It is so hard for me to say. I know I must. When I do, you will surely send me away. I could not stand to lose your friendship. I do not want you to give up on me. When I tell you what I need to…Oh Paul I have stolen. I took something that did not belong to me. At the time I did not care because I honestly felt I deserved it. I took it as though it were mine and I spent the money a long time ago. I do not have it anymore so it will be difficult for me to make it good." There he said it, but Onesimus was not feeling any better for having gotten it off his chest.

"What do you mean you stole something? I do not miss anything of any value at all. Thank you for being so honest with me, but I am not understanding at all what you mean. Please continue, if you desire." Paul was very confused with what Onesimus was needing to say.

"No, no, I would have never thought of doing such a thing since I have been blessed by the Word of God. Of course not, I would have never taken anything from you. I have seen money lying around here many times from your followers to help in your cause, but I was never once tempted to claim it for my own. You are not going to like this at all when I tell you, but it was from Philemon." On saying that, Onesimus noticed Paul's expression had turned very bleak.

Onesimus knew the thought of him having stolen from his dear friend caused Paul anguish.

"I thought when you knew that I had run away from Philemon, you would also have known that the money that was missing from him would have been taken by me. We never discussed it, but I suppose I always thought you knew it was me. I just want to be accepted and it is difficult when I have such guilt hanging over me." Onesimus wished he had shared every detail with Paul from the very beginning.

"You did not have to tell me this, but I am so grateful that you did if it helps relieve you of your anxiety. Philemon did not advise me of any money that was missing. So you stole from him while you were living there? Is that what I am hearing? What compelled you to do that, my son?" Paul was a little hurt at the thought that his special brother in the Lord had been violated.

"It actually happened the night that I left there. Although I did not plan to steal from him, I was weakened by the fact that it was made so easy for me. The temptation was right in front of me and I gave in. When I left, it was very dark and no one was around, and when I looked at the wagon that I passed as I was going down the lane, I noticed something sparkling. I ran to it and noticed a big bag of money laying right there on the wagon. It was right there for the taking! Before I knew what I was doing, my hand had already put the bag inside my garments and off I went with the money. So not only am I a runaway slave, but I am also a thief. Please know that I feel really awful. I feel so bad. I have been carrying this guilt and shame for such a long, long time that I find it hard to live with myself." Onesimus was sobbing so hard that Paul could not bear the thought of chastising him. After all, it was such a long time ago and Onesimus' heart has changed very much since that time.

"My dear son in the Lord. You are a different person now than you were then. Have you truly confessed your sin before the Lord and asked forgiveness from Him? You know that is a very important first step." Paul knew he had to turn everything around.

"No, I really did not consider that. I just didn't want to think about that part of my life. I was concentrating on moving on. I wanted to keep my eyes on the future and a life with you and Jesus." Onesimus knew now that he had to ask forgiveness in order to move on.

Paul, full of compassion, asked Onesimus to join him on his knees so they might enter into a time of prayer of forgiveness. Onesimus knelt on the hard tiled floor with Paul who asked him to repeat after him. "Father, I know I have sinned. You know it has been a long time and it has been only that once.

Please forgive my wrongdoing. I want now to have a totally clean heart and have your peace live within me. The only way I can do that is if I ask your forgiveness and in asking, I believe it will really happen. I am a sinner and unworthy of your grace. I realize that I would never be worthy, but you made it possible when you put all my sins on the cross for all time. Thank you for living inside of me. Thank you for giving me life anew in you and in knowing you. Thank you for forgiving me of this particular sin and any others that I may have committed unknowingly." Paul and Onesimus were both in tears after this tender moment together.

"I feel a total peace such as I have never felt before and I know that I have been forgiven. I am aware that my slate has been washed clean. Thank you Paul, thank you very much for leading me in the right direction. Thank you for allowing Jesus to save my soul." Onesimus was full of peace now.

"I must say that you appear to be more joyous now than you did a few minutes ago. A weight has truly been lifted. Just always remember what being close to the Lord feels like. That is what you are experiencing right now, you know. Whenever you feel like you are drifting, just remember this moment and pray earnestly to be drawn back to Him." Paul was just as excited as Onesimus to have this resolved.

He knew something else was bothering Onesimus, but he knew when the time was right, it would be disclosed.

Paul continued, "Just remember to let your conduct be worthy of the gospel of Christ. Whether I am with you or not, keep in mind that Christ lives in you. He will never leave you nor forsake you. God has highly exalted Him and given Him the name which is above every name, that at the name of Jesus every knee should bow, in heaven, in earth and under the earth. And every tongue should confess that Jesus Christ is Lord to the glory of God the Father."

"My goal is to please God and also please you. But now that you know my deep dark secret, even though I know that God has forgiven me, can you also forgive me? I know that I have let you down in knowing how sinful my past life has been." Onesimus could tell all was forgiven as far as Paul was concerned.

"Of all sinners, I, myself am the worst. The person's forgiveness you now need to seek is Philemon's," Paul clarified.

"I know that I need to ask his forgiveness also, but how am I ever going to be able to do that? I know I can do what you are always doing by writing a letter. Are you planning on sending one that way so that a messenger could take mine too?" Onesimus did not feel right about doing that, but he wanted to make restitution somehow.

"Let me have a while to think about this. I will pray and we will see where we are led. Just remember you are not the same person as you were then. We will see that Philemon realizes that as well. We all change through the grace and love of God." Paul knew he still had some reassuring to do. "Please keep in mind that I have been thrilled with the way Philemon responded to the gospel and it has gripped his heart and made him a man of love and generosity. I am aware that Philemon, Apphia, and Archippas have made their home a place of love and hospitality."

While Onesimus was in the back room preparing to run some errands for Paul, he heard a knock at the door, which was not unusual. Paul frequently had visitors such as the physician Luke and also Jesus, whom they also called Justus, who was a fellow Jew. But this was different. The voice sounded familiar.

"Greetings, Epaphras, it is so good to see you." The two men embraced each other as they kissed each other on the cheek. "I had heard that you would be coming. I am also hearing that you have been quite bold in preaching the gospel in areas where the Romans are very clear that it must not be done. I am concerned for your safety. As you are well aware, I did not listen when I was encouraged not to be so open. Epaphras, please, it will not help the cause if you are also locked up. Please be very careful."

"My dear brother Paul, I came to Rome to check on you, but I must admit that I got a little side-tracked when I came across a small church gathering and I had to join in."

"Where are my manners? Please come in and sit with me. I will have a drink and cakes brought in for your enjoyment while we talk." Paul understood Ephaphras had not seen him in chains before and realized he was quite taken aback.

"I stayed there a while to try to direct them to the right way. They had some confusion about some issues. They were having some heated discussion on judging others, which I believe I cleared up for them. I found so many people who had receptive ears that I could not restrain myself. My goal was to immediately come to you, but here I am at long last. My brother how are you? Are your needs being met.?" Epaphras looked at Paul with deep concern.

Just as Paul was about to answer, there was a loud noise from the other room. Epaphras ran to check on it for Paul and discovered a man stooped over on the floor picking up a bowl he had apparently dropped. On realizing the visitor was someone from his past, Onesimus had been startled and had dropped the bowl. "May I help you?" Ephaphras asked not knowing to whom he was addressing the question.

"No, I am taking care of this. Thank you very much but it was my carelessness that caused the mess," Onesimus answered as he got up and turned around to face the inevitable. Could it be after all these years that Epaphras would not recognize him? He had never really acknowledged him that much anyway.

"You must be the one who has been helping Paul out. Let me lend you my right hand of fellowship and may God richly bless you for your kindness." Onesimus noticed that his look was a general one and not suspicious at all. Onesimus was very relieved that he did not have to account for himself and was delighted to be shaking his hand.

Then came the affirmation. "Do I know you? You look so familiar to me like I should know you? There is a certain something in your dialect as well. May I kindly ask your name?" Epaphras began to have a flashback.

Onesimus knew he had to get it out in the open. After all, if he had the same love in his heart that Paul did, it would be all right. He was hoping it would not be an issue. "My name is Onesimus. I have been in training at the feet of Paul for quite some time now, and have delighted in being his servant here to help him out while he has been in chains."

"You know that name means 'useful one' so you have fulfilled that title. I was told by the men at the meeting that I had recently attended that Paul had a young man attending to his needs. I am very grateful to you for that. That is odd, though. My dear brother in the Lord back in Colossae, Philemon, had a young man who had run away a few years ago and he had that same name. It is just a name that I do not hear too often and he would be about your age by now. As a matter of fact you favor him immensely. I did not know Onesimus, but on occasion he brought my companions and myself refreshment while we were visiting Philemon." Epaphras was trying to put details together in his mind.

"I have been told that my name does mean 'useful one' and I am very pleased to be able to be of use to Paul." Onesimus was trying to at least answer one of his questions.

"Your accent though, it is typical for that part of the country. Are you? Could you be?" Epaphras realized he had stumbled onto something. All the while, he was trying to figure out how the runaway slave could possibly be in the home of his dear and trusted brother in the Lord, and if Paul knew this, how could he possibly keep it a secret?

"I do admit it. I am that runaway slave of Philemon's. I took off one night when I decided I needed to get away from that life. I procured a job on a ship out of Ephesus and then sailed from Athens and I ended up here. I was introduced to Paul by two fellow workers on the ship, and he has allowed me to be his hands and feet. For that opportunity I am truly grateful. You must realize that Paul did not know anything about my background until just recently and now he is trying to decide how best to deal with the situation." Once again Onesimus was relieved that he had gotten over another hurdle.

"Oh, I see you have met" Paul acknowledged as he entered the room where the conversation was being held. "Onesimus here has been a trusted servant of mine for quite some time. I do not know how I could have made it without his service to me. You know Epaphras, he is a new convert and is a child of the King now. He has put his old life behind him and is waiting for the opportune time to proclaim the gospel himself."

"Let us go back into the front room, Paul, while Onesimus here finishes cleaning up his mess." .

"Yes, we will do just that. Onesimus, will you please bring us a drink and some of those cakes you just purchased?" Paul had to get his thoughts together in order to explain the situation to his comrade.

"Epaphras, yes, let us sit here and please bring me up to date on all your travels and your ministry. I am very anxious to hear all about your adventures. You have been so steadfast in your prayers for the believers in Colossae. Please let me know how the church is doing now." Paul had a feeling that Epaphras had discerned who his visitor was but he was allowing Epaphras to comment first.

"I will certainly bring you up to date on all that momentarily, but now you have a little explaining to do for me. I have just realized who this young man is. What are you going to do? You know you cannot harbor him forever. I understand he is your right hand man, but the moral obligation you have!"

Epaphras could not believe he was being so forward with his mentor.

"I have thought all that through, Epaphras, and I have come to the conclusion that soon now I will have to correspond with Philemon and make him aware of Onesimus's presence here. It is just that he has been such an asset to me. It was only after we had bonded together that I realized the circumstances. You understand?" Paul had to make it clear that he was not really harboring a fugitive, but had come to realize that God had sent him there for a purpose.

"I definitely trust your judgment. I am sorry for being so hasty in my discernment of the situation, but I was totally caught off guard when I realized that I had come face-to-face with Philemon's slave." Epaphras understood that it would all be explained in due time.

"Thank you Onesimus for the refreshment. I certainly do not know what I would do without you." Paul wanted to instill in Epaphras what a value Onesimus had been to him and how he had become a great asset to the Cause.

"This is very delicious and a very good choice, Onesimus. I see how valuable he has become to you. That does please me so. My thoughts and prayers have been with you ever since I heard of your arrest, Paul. I am very glad you have Onesimus to help care for you," Epaphras said quite sincerely.

"Thank you for understanding. If this information got into the wrong hands, I am not sure of the consequences that would befall him, as well as me." Paul needed to make Epaphras aware of the discretion needed for this situation. "I want you to rest assured that I am praying for the direction to take in handling this situation."

"I just want to bring you up to date on my ministry that I fell into upon arriving here in Rome." Epapharas and Paul spoke together for quite some time in the front of the house while Onesimus quietly listened in from the next room. He had been trying to keep abreast of all the Christian movements around Rome. He knew how dangerous it had become to speak out about the Lord Jesus Christ. Onesimus had come to appreciate all the brave men who witnessed when they knew it could cost them their lives.

"Time has certainly gotten away from me. I had desperately needed to check on you. When I got word that you had been arrested, I had to come and see to your needs and to be sure they were all met. I will be here in Rome for a while but right now I have a group waiting for me and I must go quickly while it is calm," Epaphras explained to Paul as they embraced and he headed for the door.

"Please keep our little secret for now until I know exactly how it will be handled." Paul knew he could not let this bit of news out in the open quite yet and had to watch their wording while the guards were nearby.

"I will most assuredly do so. Peace to you, Paul," Epaphras spoke as he was going out the door.

"I will pray for your safety, but please be careful. You never know who is looking and they are quick to put a stop to the spread of the gospel," Paul said with concern in his voice as Epaphras left him and headed down the street geared up to speak about Jesus' saving grace.

"That was good for you to be open with Epaphras, Onesimus. He is a kind man and will not report back to Colossae of his meeting with you." Paul noticed that Onesimus needed some reassurance

Chapter 15

*P*aul woke up in an especially good mood on this bright sunny morning. Food had been prepared the day before and others were bringing some fresh fish in. This would be an unusual gathering and Paul could hardly contain himself. A feast! A banquet was in the making right there in Paul's rented house, commonly called his prison. The officials allowed this rare occasion and the guards had to accommodate the celebration.

The first guest to arrive was Tychicus, and following him were Demas and Luke "Greetings my dear brothers. It is so very good to have you sup with me today." Paul was very elated to have them visit.

The next to arrive were Jesus, called Justus, and Aristarchus and Mark, who were Paul's only Jewish fellow workers for the Lord there in Rome.

Then came Epaphras, so the numbers were complete and the supper could begin. All of Paul's close friends and encouragers were gathered together under one roof. What a day! What a celebration! It happened that each of these good men were in Rome at the same time and able to be here. "What a splendid day!" Paul was beside himself with joy. "The only thing that would make this event more perfect would be if Jesus Christ Himself could descend down upon us."

The fellowship was good. Many hours of conversation went by with each one telling of their particular ministry while in Rome and their recent travels. It was exciting to hear of their spreading the gospel and to know that lives had been changed. Onesimus was part of the group but was more of an observer and felt honored to be in the presence of such godly men — men who were risking their lives for the Cause.

Luke told stories of traveling with Paul to Philippi and how encouraged they were to see a group of women having their own worship service by the river's edge.

Upon learning that Onesimus had spent a great deal of time on the sea, Luke also told of some of the times he accompanied Paul and shared the time they sailed to Troas together.

"I would like for everyone to know that Demas has been a very valuable companion to me and fellow laborer with me while I have been imprisoned here in Rome. His time spent with me here has been most reassuring." Paul just felt like lifting up some of the people who were a blessing to him.

"I cannot say enough about Tychicus who has been such an encourager to me and he has traveled in areas where I have not been able to go. He has been sending messages to me from great distances and brings me back reports of converts for whom I have much concern." Paul continued in his praises.

"Aristachus, it is so good to be with you in a very peaceful setting. It seems we have stirred up trouble everywhere we have traveled together. I am so mindful of the time in Ephesus where you and Gaius were seized in the theatre. That was one instance where their confusion was to your advantage. They really wanted me, and I suppose you were a temporary distraction to them at the time." Paul has had lots of time to think of his past encounters and is so glad to have these men here to share special thoughts.

"John Mark," Paul spoke with a little hesitancy in his voice, "you and I have known each other for a very long time. Even though we were estranged for a few years, it is good that we are fellow workers once more. When we first met, you were young just like Onesimus was when I first was introduced to him. He has become very valuable to me, and Mark you also. I often speak of the mountains we had to climb in order to be where we now are."

"Justus has been a great comfort to me. There have been times that I have felt so abandoned, but I can always count on

Justus to be there for me. He has been a loyal encourager in the faith." Paul noticed the tears in his friends' eyes as he spoke.

Paul realized that repeating himself never hurt anything so he added, "Believers are God's workmanship created in Christ Jesus to do good works, which God prepared in advance for us to do. Be sure and know that repetition is always an asset in teaching the Word of God. If your students of the faith do not get it the first time, then maybe they will when spoken again."

"Always preach the Word and avoid useless disputes. I dislike babblings that cause so much dissension in the church and takes so much time to repair. As you go out, I would like to see that you model a right approach, that of a tested spiritual laborer, which each of you are. Please do not be ashamed of the work you are doing or how you perform it." When Paul spoke to these faithful men, he spoke as though he may not have another opportunity to be with them.

Each man had a very unique quality and approach to sending out the gospel. It was apparent they were all so eager to do what they could while in the sinful city of Rome to establish Christian core groups to better branch out. Any one of them could have been captured and taken prisoner, just like Paul.

After their farewells were spoken, Paul was exhausted, but before he could sleep, he would pray and study. Every night he would spend hours in solitude praying, meditating and reading from the Pentateuch or other passages from the Testament. This night was no different. He would spend countless hours on this particular night in prayer for his brothers; for their safety and that their message would fall on fertile hearts and ears.

After several days, Onesimus continued to speak of how much he enjoyed having dinner with such honored guests. He was refreshed to listen to their stories and the narrow brushes they had had with death. Each of them had their own ministry and was not hampered in anyway of continuing with their mission. As Paul and Onesimus were sharing their thoughts of that evening, there was a sudden disruption.

"What is that noise I hear outside the door Onesimus? Could you please check for me?" Onesimus quickly went to the door, but one of the guards on duty got there first and found soldiers escorting Aristachus into the house. They gave him a push as he fell on the floor in front of Paul

"Here, you enjoy each other so much, now you can spend quality time together," a guard scoffed sarcastically as he took pleasure in seeing Aristachus lie on the floor with scratches on his face. "Meet your new roommate. He is going to be with you for a while."

"Let me help you up," Onesimus said, feeling so sorry that this had to happen to a new friend.

"Please tell me what has happened to you. Where were you? What provoked the arrest?" Paul was anxious to hear all about it.

"I was speaking in front of the tables where change was being made for paying of the taxes. I spoke up very boldly for the way the poor people were being treated. They were greatly cheating them and had no reservations in doing so right there in front of everyone. I made them aware of Jesus and how they were using their authority to swindle the children of God. I went on just as you would have done, and I was given a prompt and speedy trial and here I am." Aristachus shared his adventure with the two men. "Paul, I count it a privilege to be in your company and suffer with you."

"Your charge does not sound as harsh as mine. We will pray that you will be released very soon," Paul said with confidence.

Chapter 16

o the days went by with Paul and Aristachus both imprisoned in the rented house with freedom to move around, and on occasion, receive visitors and write. At times there would be a believing traveler stop in to visit with them, instill encouragement, and leave them with the knowledge that they would be continuously lifted up in prayer.

On one of these days, soon after a believer had left, Paul knew there was a very important subject he needed to approach with Onesimus. It was not an easy subject to bring up, but had been neglected much too long already.

"Onesimus, please sit with me. I do need to run something past you." Paul looked very serious as he motioned for Onesimus to sit near him. "I believe it to be time, my dear brother, to write a letter to our beloved Philemon as to your whereabouts. I have felt convicted that it is the time to do so. Please do not be alarmed for I feel confident that he will

Freedom Revealed

receive this information very peacefully. Please let me know if you feel uncomfortable at all in me doing so at this time."

"I have truly been expecting this conversation to take place at any moment. I, too, think that the time has come to do so. Do what you must do and you will have my approval. I know you have been given a gift of articulation and you will guard your words very carefully; therefore, I trust in your judgment." Onesimus could not believe the calmness he felt in getting this done.

"I have been in the process of writing to the church in Colossae and I will be completing one to the church in Ephesus. These could all be delivered at the same time. I just need to think how we might accomplish that." Paul knew what needed to happen but did not want to spring all the news on Onesimus at the same time.

"Would it be too bold for me to ask you if I can be the one to take the letter to him? I feel that by your writing the letter and having someone else take it that would make me appear a coward. I feel very strong about this. Please advise me." Onesimus was not sure what the best course of action would be, but he knew he would need to eventually face Philemon.

"Why, Onesimus, I am surprised that you would volunteer for such a mission, but I must say that you are mature enough in the faith to face whatever is ahead, and I am quite taken aback that you would offer to do it." Paul was so proud of his

194

son in the faith. He was very pleased that he would come forth and offer to go to Philemon himself.

Paul felt as though he must add, "Now that you have been converted, the principles of Christian teaching would require you to return, but the conditions of your return will be explained in this letter that I will write and compose very affectionately. You would be returning as a servant, but more than that 'a brother beloved both in the flesh and in the Lord'. Hopefully, Philemon will desire to receive you in this tender appeal in consciousness of how much he owes to me in my asking. I will be reminding Philemon that you are my own son in the Gospel, as well as myself."

"I have come a long way because of you, and my strength has been revealed from you. You have shown me that through Jesus Christ everything is possible. I realize it is a long, hard trip in itself, much less the agonizing thought of wondering how my former master will receive me." Onesimus was not ruling out what could face him. "I made the trip over here when I was much younger, so I feel confident I can do it again."

"He is not your former master, you know. He is truly still your master. I have been harboring you from him for quite some time now. For that I trust he will understand. We must be very careful how we word this message to him and pray for guidance in preparing the letter he will receive. Let us also pray that he will be benevolent to the messenger as well, whether it be a friend or especially if it be you." Paul wanted to make it clear to Onesimus that his allegiance still should remain to Philemon.

"You have taught me to pray but not only in just speaking words, but to pray believing that my prayers will be heard and answered. I will commit to the Lord the entire situation, praying for direction if I am to be the one to go or not. I will pray for wisdom and for your clarity in writing the letter. I will pray for a receptive heart in Philemon as he reads the letter from you. I will pray for safety for the person who makes the big trip to deliver it to Philemon's door." Onesimus was trying his best to pray specifically as Paul had taught him and not to omit any important details in this crucial encounter.

"Thank you. You have grown deeply in the faith and it is very touching for me to hear you speak so forthrightly. Let me just have some time alone now so that I might compose this important document." Paul spoke with a heavy heart as he took his pen in hand and began to put the letter together.

While Paul had just taken pen in hand, Timothy appeared at the door and was greeted affectionately by Onesimus. He spoke with Timothy on the decision that had been made on composing the letter and that Paul had just begun the process.

"Paul, is there anything I can do to help you with this, what I would presume to be, difficult composition?" Timothy asked knowing how difficult it was anymore for Paul to do his own writing.

The afternoon went by very slowly for Onesimus. He had kept himself busy with the duties that had been assigned to him earlier in the day. The evening meal had been delivered by a friend and when Paul, Onesimus, and Aristachus came together, no one spoke a word for a while. Aristachus had by now been totally informed of Onesimus's past life and the circumstances that brought him to this point. It was hard for Aristachus to believe that he had been a deceiver since all he could see in Onesimus was purity and love for his fellow man. The two men were waiting for Paul to let them know if he had finished the letter or even the possibility that he may have been led not to even compose it.

"I want to share with you what I felt led to say to the church at Ephesus in the letter that I have been writing to them. Philemon, because of the time we have spent together, I have new thoughts on the relationship between masters and slaves. There have been slaves in the Ephesian church who have become believers and I want to tell them to be sure and show respect to their masters and that it needs to come from their heart. They need to know that they should work at all times as if they are being watched whether they are or not and to not take advantage just because they are now new believers. Also, on the other side of the situation, I am informing the masters to treat their slaves in a right manner and not to keep threatening them."

"The letter to Philemon is finished with the help of Timothy who did the writing for me. Onesimus, I feel that the Holy Spirit led me to write a letter that Philemon will receive quite nicely. I do not feel we should delay. As much as it pains me to say this, I believe that you should leave the day after tomorrow. I understand that is the best day to catch a ship out to head toward the east and will get you to your destination in a timely fashion. It would be better for all concerned if you do not travel alone. Did Tychicus say when he was by here that he would be needing to go to Ephesus shortly?" Paul tried not to show his sorrow in giving his suggestions because he would be losing a great deal by sending Onesimus off.

Aristachus tried to bring a little brightness to an otherwise somber table. "You heard correctly; Tychicus plans to go there soon and who better than he would make such an amazing traveling companion."

"I am feeling a bit weary tonight. Onesimus, could you please locate him and have him come to me first thing in the morning so that we may discuss this. I will go to my room now. I need this time to meditate and trust in the Lord's guidance."

Paul was exhausted from pouring so much of himself into this emotional letter he had just compiled-- a letter written to his dear friend and brother in the Lord in disclosing the truth, all the while hoping Philemon would be forgiving and receptive to Onesimus.

Tychicus arrived with Onesimus the next morning without realizing the reason why. He did notice Onesimus to be a little more anxious than usual.

"Is there a particular reason you are so quiet this morning?" Tychicus asked of Onesimus, "You are usually very chipper."

"You will soon be told the news that concerns the two of us." Onesimus wanted Paul to be the one to tell Tychicus the plans.

"Good morning, my dear brother and welcome. Please come in, sit and I will see that you have a drink and some bread." Paul greeted Tychicus just like always.

"It is a joyous blessing to come and see you. I consider my time with you very precious and fulfilling. Is there anything in particular I may do for you today?" Tychicus asked seeing that Paul's look had turned to concern.

"You spoke the other day that you were considering making a trip to Ephesus, is that correct?" Paul wanted to hear his current plans before he brought up his agenda.

"I have not made definite plans, but I should be heading out soon. I really do not have anything to keep me here. Unless I may serve you in any particular way?" Tychicus read right through Paul and knew something was going on.

"How about leaving on the ship that heads out tomorrow? Could you go then? I have some letters to churches in that area and would love for them to be received before too long. I do want them to be aware of some issues and have plans for you to not go alone. I have a trusted traveling companion chosen to go with you." Paul was careful to spring the news to him gently since Tychicus was not aware of what was going on here.

"You know I do not especially enjoy traveling so far alone and I would welcome someone to go with me. Who do you have in mind? And why so soon? Tomorrow is very soon." Tychicus's curiosity was getting the best of him.

"The person that would be traveling with you is Onesimus. He has business in Colossae, and I have composed a letter, which is to be given to Philemon who lives in that town. You have heard me speak of him I am sure. I have a letter to the church in Ephesus and also to the Colossians. This trip needs to be made expeditiously. So do we have your agreement in all the plans as you now know them? Can you be ready to leave tomorrow?" Paul gathered that Tychicus was looking a little curious but he was always very cooperative any time Paul asked a favor.

"I will be ready to leave tomorrow. If I remember the schedule correctly, the ship leaves around 8:00 in the morning. But then, knowing you, you are already aware of that. Please allow me today to finish up some things I have going and I will be at your front door first thing in the morning. We will leave together then, Onesimus." Tychicus felt he was still left in the dark, but knew whatever he needed to know had been told him.

Paul spent as much quality time with Onesimus as the day had to offer. He wanted to instill in Onesimus some thoughts that he should carry along.

"I pray that you might be active in sharing your faith so that you will have a full understanding of every good thing you have in Christ. Sharing faith in Christ has to do with sharing the good which Christ is endeavoring to implant in us all. It has to do with sharing the love of Christ with each other through how we interact with each other. Just as Philemon's faith has strengthened the entire community of Colossae, so Onesimus, your faith will impact the relationships of others there as well. Faith grows as a living faith is shared. True forgiveness will come as you forgive others. Your faith in God's forgiveness will grow as you share that forgiveness with others. That being said I feel confident of Philemon's forgiveness to you. I trust in Philemon's love of Christ to lead him to do the right thing." Paul was strengthened by his own words.

Onesimus had a rather restless night. It had been a long time since he had traveled on the open sea and he was feeling a little apprehensive. He felt as though once again he was losing his security. He had come to rely on Paul for so many things, being his trusted companion, teacher, mentor, prayer partner, and family for quite some time now.

Paul, too, did not sleep well. He was reluctant in letting Onesimus go, but knew in his heart that it had to be done. Paul decided that he should also include some suggestions to the church at Colossae since he had done so with the Ephesians. He wanted to emphasize to the slaves who had become believers there to be obedient to their earthly masters not only because they want to please them, but also since they have love for the Lord. 'You are to work hard and with a cheerful heart, remembering that Christ will be the one in the end that will give you your eternal reward. You slave owners must be just and fair to your slaves remembering that you have a Master in heaven who is closely watching you.' If it wasn't for his time spent in sharing with Onesimus the life of a slave, he would not have considered including this.

He depended on Onesimus in so many areas. He was like a son to him. He ran errands, helped around the house, assembled meetings, managed the meals when none was furnished, encouraged him when he felt a little down, inspired him in some of his writings. What a faithful servant! Now that was going to come to an end.

There was a knock at the door and as Tychicus came in carrying his bag, he was greeted by two men who looked quite somber. They attempted to each acknowledge Tychicus with a smile on their face, but deep down they were grieving. They were both trying to be brave for each other, realizing that they may not see each other again. What a loss for them to understand that their parting may be forever.

"I just want you to know, Onesimus, that I guarded the wording of this letter very carefully. I did not use the term 'runaway', but rather my choice of words was 'separated from'. I am aware that in case this letter got in the wrong hands, it might jeopardize your safety. There would be no use to take unnecessary chances." Paul felt he needed to reassure Onesimus.

"That is good thinking. I do not know what was written, but I have been assured you are careful in all words," Onesimus said as he gave Paul his last hug and kiss.

"My son, please do not forget me. Do not stray from the Lord you have come to know so well. He is closer to you than a brother and will always be with you," Paul said, trusting that his words were more an assurance for himself.

Paul, Timothy, Onesimus, Tychicus and Artistachus gathered in a circle and had a lengthy prayer together before the two departed. Paul reminded him of the passage they once read together that is taken from the book of Joshua: 'Do not be terrified. Do not be discouraged, for the Lord your God will be with you wherever you go'.

It was a long, hard day for Paul after bidding the two men good-bye. Paul felt as though a part of himself had left. It was not the first time he had been a faithful father figure to a young man such as Onesimus. But there was a certain bond he had with him that he could not explain. This was the first time he had come this far with anyone while being in chains and depended so much on that person. He only trusted that he would receive word of their safety soon after their arrival in Colossae.

Onesimus walked down the path carrying his heavy bag, but it was not nearly as heavy as his own heart was at that moment. He turned to give Paul one last look before leaving his sight.

"I get the feeling that you believe you will never see Paul again. Is this a permanent move you are making?" Tychicus could not wait any longer to know a little of what was going on.

"I feel that way as much as I have ever felt anything in my life. I believe that this parting is for all time. I somehow have the impression that I will never be face to face with Paul again and that saddens me," Onesimus shared with Tychicus.

"Then why are you leaving since it seems to be so hard on the two of you? Why not just stay here and be an asset to each other?" Tychicus just had to get this settled.

"I will tell you in due time what brought all this about and why I must go to Colossae. There is a greater reason why I need to leave than any selfish reason on my part of why I should remain here. Although staying would be far easier." Onesimus could not bring himself to say anymore.

They arrived at the pier, paid for their passage and boarded the ship as Onesimus realized this would be a far different feeling than he had ever had on the seas before. This was the first time he was a paying passenger and it felt very good not to have to be at the mercy of the men he had to work along-side. He was assuring himself that this would be a much more peaceful voyage. He sat down next to Tychicus to relax and enjoy the view of the city of Rome as they departed from it. He realized it did not look nearly as large to him as it had when he arrived. Tychicus shared with Onesimus some of the trips he had taken, mainly those in service to Paul. He had several occurrences when he was close to death, many times he had been cursed, and several times he had to run for his life.

"Being a servant for the Lord is not always the easy path to take, although you would think it would not be that way. Did Paul ever tell you that I traveled with him from Macedonia to

Jerusalem before he came to Rome?" Tychicus was wanting to draw closer to Onesimus by sharing his life with him.

"I believe he did mention that, but since it was before I met you, I really did not connect it was you. Please tell me some of the stories of your traveling together. I must say, Paul really has a lot of stamina for a man his age." Onesimus did not know if he had said the wrong thing or not by the expression on Tychicus' face.

"Paul is really not as old as you may think he is. He has led a pretty rugged life when you think about it. I do not know if he has told you about all the times he had been beaten and had stones thrown at him. He has escaped danger many times. The energy spent on all his travels has been enough to age anyone. The one thing that has kept him going is the inner joy and also the peace that he has." Tychicus wanted to be certain Onesimus knew the struggles Paul had had in his life since he was converted.

"No, he did not tell me too much about his hard times. He always made his life seem so fulfilled and joyous that I would never have thought it had been that much of a hardship." Onesimus was sad to hear about Paul's encounters.

"He does not talk about that side since he focuses on the positive. I just wanted you to be aware since I was confident he did not use his time with you to focus on himself." Tychicus was aware Onesimus was having a hard time with the fact that Paul had done so much suffering.

Tychicus told of his opportunities in his own life and all about his encounters. The time went quickly and suddenly, they had a day's journey behind them.

"Have you gotten your sea legs back, Onesimus?" Tychicus greeted him after a good night of rest

"I did rest fairly well last evening, and the sun is shining brightly bringing us into a new day. It is amazing how we can see no land at all. This is all God's handiwork. The beautiful sunrise, sparkling water as far as you can possibly see, and right now all is peaceful with the world." Onesimus was amazed at how calm he actually was.

"Why don't we get the day started by my hearing about you and what you have accomplished so far in your still young life? I shared many of my experiences with you yesterday, now it is your turn today." Tychicus sat back awaiting Onesimus's story.

"My life has not been nearly as exciting as yours. And certainly not as blessed. I could tell you my history, but I am afraid you will not like what you hear, and you certainly will not think very highly of me after it has been told." Onesimus was not sure if he wanted to go into too much detail or not.

"Well, let me be the judge of that, will you? We still have lots of time on this ship together, then a lot of miles on foot before our journey comes to an end. Just share whatever you want to share with me; I am not going anywhere." Tychicus knew there was a secret inside of Onesimus but knew he would tell his only if he felt led to do so.

After a few minutes went by, Onesimus decided there would be no better time than the present to open up to Tychicus and let him know all the details of his past life. It was strange that during Onesimus's confessions, Tychicus did not seem surprised by anything he heard. He was so understanding and compassionate. "Is this God's grace? Is this what it means to have a pure heart? How can anyone sit through my life story and not be judgmental?" Onesimus wondered.

"You have had a most interesting life so far, and I thought your story was going to be boring. I would say it was far from that, but to think, Onesimus, you have had quite a burden to carry around with you for such a long time and for that I am truly sorry. I can only imagine the thought of someone–anyone actually hating me. That would be a lot to bear. I can see how you need to get this resolved so that you can begin living a really fulfilled life. Until you put this entire issue behind you, you cannot serve Christ whole-heartedly." Compassion filled Tychicus as he assured Onesimus.

"That is it? You are not going to demean me or tell me what a bad person I am for turning on a very godly man?" Onesimus was having a hard time understanding Tychicus's calmness.

"It is not for me to judge. I believe that since you have met Paul, you have found restitution. This has not changed my feelings for you in any way and you are no less a man to me. We all make mistakes throughout our lives. Yours came at a young age and before you walked with the Lord. That makes all the difference in the world." Tychicus always had a way of making people feel very much at ease. "However, I cannot determine what Philemon's response will be."

"I am so glad now that I have shared this with you so that I can really enjoy the rest of the trip." As Onesimus spoke to Tychicus, he now was assured that he was not going to be at full peace until he came face to face with Philemon.

The trip did not seem as long as Onesimus had anticipated it would. How strange it was to be traveling on the waters and not be a part of the crew. He tried his best to just relax and enjoy this 'down' time not knowing what life would be like once he arrived at Philemon's door. Onesimus did feel somewhat better after sharing his past life with Tychicus; at least the story and the questions helped pass the time away. He was amazed how understanding Tychicus was especially when he added that he might have done exactly the same thing. He understood why Paul enjoyed having Tychicus as part of his fellowship of believers; he was such an encourager and that is a trait that Onesimus wanted to emulate.

"We are almost to Cnidus so we will soon have to make a decision. Do we go on to Colossae with me staying a few days with you to be sure you are all right, and then I will go back to Ephesus to deliver the letter there, or do we both go to Ephesus and then we go on to Colossae? What is your pleasure, Onesimus? I am afraid that once you get to Colossae then you might just be there for a long while and it may do you some good to make the extra little venture up to Ephesus first." Tychicus was not sure if Onesimus wanted to stretch out his trip or have his encounter with Philemon over with as soon as possible.

"Well I have not thought it through since I was leaving all this planning up to you, but are you fearing that perchance Philemon may have me arrested or put me back in bondage? Is that why you inferred that I might be there for a long time and should take advantage of my freedom while I have it?" Onesimus asked with a worried look.

"Oh, no, not at all. That is not what I meant so please do not jump to conclusions about what Philemon might do. Remember that it has been such a long time since you have left and he is a very pure man and will do the right thing in God's eyes," Tychicus responded.

"I do have a favor then to ask you. I am fairly knowledge-able of the lay of the land, after having traveled that route before, and if I remember correctly, there is a little town called Miletus that would not be too far out of our way. Do you know its location?" Onesimus hesitantly asked.

"Yes, I have been there on occasion and it is not much out of our way if we head toward Ephesus first. I must say, you have me curious as to why you would ask about that little village." Tychicus was inquisitive at this point. "Did you know that is where Paul once met the elders of the church of Ephesus after calling them together in order to save time in his departure as he was headed to Jerusalem and wanted to be there in time for Pentecost?"

"No, that never came up in conversation and I really wish it had. Anyway, I became acquainted with a very lovely family who resides in Miletus. I am fairly certain they are still there, and it would ease my mind to check on them. The day after I left Philemon's home, I met up with them and we became traveling companions until we reached their home in Miletus. They were very kind to me and such a big help when I had no place to turn. It would be so nice to see how they are doing after all this time. I am in their debt and I would love more than anything to be able to visit with them for a while." Onesimus was feeling excited at the thought of seeing Tisha and Julian again.

After Onesimus filled Tychicus in on his entire time spent with them, Tychicus was delighted to go out of his way and be able to meet them himself.

"That would be just fine. It has been a very long time since I have been to Miletus and I also know someone there. This will also give me a chance to renew an old acquaintance. After we get our belongings together, we will still have a big part of the day when we get there. That will be a lovely place for us to stay if you think it will not be too much of an imposition. We could get an early start for Ephesus the next morning unless you need more time than that to get caught up. I am rather anxious to meet these people who befriended you."

"It is hard to get rid of our sea legs, so we need to get some walking in. Think you can make the physical trip by foot all the way?" Tychicus asked, even though Onesimus was in much better shape than he was.

"I certainly will not have a problem traveling this relatively short distance since I am so full of anticipation in seeing these people again. This is not a trip I am dreading." Onesimus was relieved to be able to prolong the 'homecoming' at Philemon's a little longer.

"I believe there is more in Miletus than just an acquaintance. Somehow I am discerning that there is someone, this Tisha you talked about, and that perchance she could be really special to you." Tychicus enjoyed teasing with Onesimus every chance he got.

"Could be. However it has been a long time and a lot has happened since then." Onesimus did not know what he would find there, but was anxious to find out.

"I am totally up for the entire trip physically, but as we get closer to Colossae, I am not sure if I can handle the emotional and mental aspects. I know that I deserve anything that comes my way from my master. It was bad enough that I ran away, but when I think that I stole from him, I cannot believe that I did such a thing." Onesimus knew that in a couple of days now he would find out.

Chapter 17

As Onesimus walked down the street toward the house where Tisha's sister lived, he noticed that a boy was playing in front of the house. As he approached he wondered if it could possibly be Julian. If so, he had changed quite a bit since last he had seen him.

"Is your name Julian?" Onesimus asked, realizing as he got a closer look that it had to be.

"Yes, that is correct. Do you want to play marbles with me?" The boy asked as his mother came to the door.

"Tisha, it is so good to see you. How are you doing?" Onesimus was so happy to see her again.

"Onesimus, is that you? Why, I have recently been thinking of you, wondering how you were doing and where you were." Tisha was just as thrilled to see him as he was to see her.

"My apologies to you for taking off so abruptly, but the ship would not wait. I was so honored to be asked to be part of the crew that I had no choice but to depart immediately. I felt really bad that I did not come in person to say good-bye, but I did send a messenger to you with my plans of sailing to Rome. I could not have passed up that opportunity" Onesimus told Tisha apologetically.

"I understand. I had reports of your whereabouts for a while; however, then I lost track, so I feel very relieved in seeing you now," Tisha said with pleasure.

"Please forgive me for my bad manners. This is Tychicus who has been my traveling companion since we left Paul in Rome. Tychicus, this is my friend, Tisha and little Julian. Tychicus and I have many things in common and we would like the opportunity to bring you up to date." Onesimus wanted to share his past life with her.

"No, please forgive me. Come in and I will give you a drink. You must be very tired and hungry as I presume you came by the boat that just arrived. Let me see what I can find to share with you. Can I make your old bed up for you upstairs so that you may spend some time with us?" Tisha was hoping Onesimus would be able to be with her for a while. "What about you, Tychicus, can you stay as well? Travelers who stop in to worship here always know they have a bed awaiting them and we would be more than happy to have you."

"I would be honored to stay with you for the night, but I know someone who lives a few streets over and I will go there if that meets with his plans." Tychicus was quite entertained in watching the two share their experiences and bring each other up to date since they had last seen each other.

After what seemed like hours of getting caught up on what had been going on in their lives, Tisha needed to be enlightened.

"You keep mentioning Paul and your relationship with him. Could this be the same Paul of Tarsus that I have also heard so much about? My sister's husband has talked of a Paul who spoke here not too awfully long ago." Tisha was curious to know since she realized he would have been a very strong force in Onesimus's life.

"Well yes. So you are aware of him as well?" With a nod of Tisha's head, Onesimus continued. "I am very thrilled to know that since I had not realized until Tychicus had told me on the trip down that Paul had been here. I gather he made quite an impression."

"He stopped here one time that I am aware of. He apparently did not want to go on to Ephesus, but did need to meet with some people, and that meeting was held here in our little seaport town. At that time, some of the new Christians had the opportunity to see him. I was encouraged to know that my brother-in-law got to go see him and even though he stood far in the back of the crowd, he realized what a dynamic man of God he was. That brief encounter changed his life, so I can only imagine how being with him for such a long period of time would have impacted your life as well." Tisha spoke with such enthusiasm she could hardly restrain herself.

Realizing they needed time alone, Tychicus decided it was time to seek out his old friend. Tisha then gave him directions on where the friend now lived and invited him back if the man was not home.

"See you in the morning, Onesimus. Thank you for your hospitality, Tisha." Tychicus said as he turned to the right and went up a little hill in search of his old friend.

"It has been such a long time since we have seen each other, and you can see for yourself that my little boy has grown so much." Tisha was very excited to see this man who she had spent brief but quality time with in her past.

Onesimus and Tisha talked quite late into the evening, filling each other in about so much of their lost time together. Then the rest of her family walked in the door.

Looking startled to see guests in their home, they realized at once who it was.

"Onesimus, what a surprise to see you. I am delighted you have found your way here after such a very long time. Are you all right? What have you been doing since we lost track of you?" Tamara excitedly asked.

"It is good to see you again also. I have been living in Rome and am going to Colossae where I have business to conduct there." As Onesimus spoke he rose from his chair to give Tamara and her husband a gracious hug.

"Tamara, you will never believe who Onesimus has been keeping company with while in Rome. Remember Paul who you listened to while he was here briefly? Yes, the same Paul of Tarsus. Can you believe it?" Tisha could not contain herself to share this kind of news with her family.

"What an honor for you! Please tell us all about how the two of you met and how you got from Athens to Rome?" Tamara was just as excited as Tisha to be able to hear about Onesimus's special companion.

Even though it was getting very late, they continued their conversation about Onesimus' life and his quality time spent at the feet of Paul.

"We are very pleased for you and can see that there has been a very big change made in your life. It is easy to see that God has been living inside of you and we are delighted in that you had the influence of Paul on your life. God needs more good men working for Him and I can tell that you are one of them." Tamara could tell there was something great in store for this young man.

"How was your trip to Samos? I trust you had a nice visit with Theta and her family? I know you must be exhausted as well." Tisha asked of Tamara, who had just returned with her husband from visiting their other sister who had recently moved there.

"It was a wonderful trip and we went at the right season for their olives. Look at the bounty we brought back." Tamara was happy to show off this blessing.

"We need to get our rest now and continue the conversation in the morning when we will all be fresh. I have made Onesimus's old bed ready upstairs. I hope that you do not mind, Tamara."

Jeremiah and Tamara assured her it was an honor for them to have Onesimus as their guest.

Onesimus knew he could have stayed up all night laughing and talking with Tisha. They seemed to have so much to share together taking up right where they left off so long ago. Onesimus thought how he really hated to leave so soon and not have a longer visit, but knew he could not tarry much longer in meeting with Philemon.

Bright and early the next morning there was a knock at the door as Onesimus, Tisha and Julian were finishing their breakfast. "Good morning to everyone on this beautiful day." Tychicus greeted them knowing it might be difficult to pull Onesimus away from all this.

"Good morning, Tychicus. Have you had breakfast already this morning?" Tisha asked hoping he had not so he might join them and be able to lengthen their time with her.

"Actually, I have not. My friends were not up yet. We said our good-byes last night and I left too early for them." As Tychicus spoke, Tisha began preparing a plate for him.

"This will not delay you too much and you will have a hot meal to begin the trip." Tisha said to Tychicus as she placed the plate before him.

Tychicus was reading her very clearly and decided that a few minutes would not make much difference. "You are much too kind. I am very appreciative of your hospitality".

After breakfast was finished. the time had come to leave. "Thank you again for all that you have done. If at all possible, I will visit with you again. We must be on our way now. May God bless you and all your family." As Onesimus embraced Tisha, he could not help but notice a tear had appeared in the corner of her eye.

"I too am grateful for the wonderful breakfast. You are a very good cook and hospitality is one of your virtues. So long, little fellow," Tychicus spoke as he rubbed the top of Julian's head.

"I wish you did not have to leave so soon. You only just got here. Can you not wait a few more days?" Tisha asked.

"I am so sorry. I wish I could stay longer. We are headed for Ephesus and then on to Colossae so this was a very good stop for us. If it is up to me, I will be back to see you very soon. There are things that are not in my control, so I am not sure what is in my future." Onesimus knew his life was not his own after he left here, but he could not share any more with Tisha.

Julian began to cry at the thought of his newfound friend leaving him so soon. That certainly did not help matters as they were saying good-bye.

"Please travel carefully. God bless both of you." Tisha spoke as she wiped more than the one tear away.

"Thank you so much for being so hospitable and for the basket of food that you prepared for us. This will keep us energized for the road ahead." Tychicus added.

During the thirty-mile trip from Miletus to Ephesus, Onesimus endured quite a bit of ribbing from Tychicus regarding his reacquainted "friend". "That joking around was just what I needed at this time," Onesimus thought to himself.

The trip was very uneventful. They met just a few people walking along the way during their journey. It was a very full day of walking, but they made excellent time which was due to the fact they were well-rested and the terrain was quite manageable. "Of course it helps by not having a little one along as was the issue before for me," Onesimus shared.

The time spent in Ephesus was most rewarding for Onesimus. He had been there before while he was working on the boats, but it did not have the same impact as it did after his time spent with Paul. He retraced steps that Paul must have taken and ventured into the synagogue where Paul boldly spoke for a few months. Onesimus found his way to the lecture hall of Tyrannus where all the Greeks and Jews of Asia had the opportunity to hear Paul's words. What a fantastic city!

"I have the letter delivered. Shall we be off to Colossae?" Tychicus could tell Onesimus had enjoyed his time spent in Ephesus.

"I have been trying to visualize Paul being here and speaking to so many people. I can only imagine the enthusiasm that he would have had as he spoke to the crowds of people and individuals as well. Paul shared with me often of his time here. You know he stayed here well over two years. That was quite a lot of time for him to have been in one place." Onesimus spoke to Tychicus as if he were unaware of Paul's ministry.

As they sat together on the stone by the fountain, they spoke of the relationships that Paul had while he was in Ephesus. "While here, Paul molded many lives and trained a lot of leaders for Him as he was called to feed Christ's sheep serving in humility of mind and never thinking of himself. He knew that only by allowing the Holy Spirit to work through him could the Lord's service be accomplished. Paul is still determined that he will finish the work God has given him with joy, triumphantly. In this place, he taught publicly as well as from house to house and not allowing opposition to affect his work. We can understand that when Paul last met with the Ephesians, the time Tamara and Tisha spoke of in Miletus, how they must have wept. They could not bear to see him go, but they also had great joy because a deep love was there. It was this quality of love to their Lord and to each other and also to the needy that distinguished the Ephesian church from all others." Tychicus shared as they sat together sharing stories of Paul.

"I continue to be impressed by his representation." Onesimus had grown in the faith just while being in Ephesus. "I understand that evangelism here was very explosive and unpredictable. There were people who came here from a lot of different backgrounds. I remember him telling me that his dear friends, Aquila and Priscilla traveled with him here as well."

"That is very true, and Paul was most effective here; many witnessed his healing of the sick and curing diseases. There were also several 'health professionals' including one group known as the seven sons of Sceva who attempted to imitate Paul through rituals. The incident produced a lot more converts to Christianity driving occult practitioners out of business. The growing community of believers lit a bonfire and destroyed magic books valued at thousands of hours of wages.

"I also know that Paul had good times of sharing with the Jews and Greeks alike while here. I am well aware that he had quite a few challenges here too," Tychicus said as they left the large city.

Chapter 18

When they saw Philemon's home in view, Onesimus's heart started to beat very fast. "Can I do this? Can I actually go to the door, knock on it, and really meet Philemon face to face? What is he going to do? Will he even take time to read the wonderful letter Paul composed before he becomes overcome with hostility? How upset will he be? Will he take Paul's word for it? Will he even listen to Paul?" Onesimus was struggling with emotions.

If Tychicus was ever an encourager now was the time. "Onesimus, please remember that Philemon is a man of the Lord. He is a believer and a very strong one. He has led so many people to Christ, and he realizes that there will be people watching to see how he will handle this particular situation. When we give him the letter from Paul addressed specifically to him, he will be so overjoyed to receive it, that of course he will open it and read it before he does anything else."

"Oh I hope that you are right." Onesimus seemed a little more assured. "I am walking in faith and do not know what I would do without it right now. My future and my entire life are hanging in the balance depending on Philemon's decision."

"Keep in mind that as soon as I know how things are going here, I must get this other letter delivered. Let me give you one last embrace before we make that knock on the door," Tychicus said, trusting all would be all right. Just then the door was opened by a servant who called Philemon to come and greet his guests.

"Greetings, I remember your being with Paul when he spoke in Ephesus a while back, but please refresh me on your name. I must say I am very taken aback by your being here, but who is accompanying you?" Philemon gave Tychicus the traditional embrace as he asked. Onesimus could tell that Philemon had not recognized him. "There is something familiar about you, but I am not clear what it is," he said as he turned to Onesimus. "Please have a seat and tell me what brings you here."

"Actually, we have a letter that we are bringing to you from Paul, who is in prison, or rather house arrest in Rome. He wanted me to be sure that, before you read it, you prayerfully consider its contents and to receive it and this dear brother here as you would Paul himself if he were the one with us now." Tychicus set the tone.

After reading the letter, Philemon looked at Onesimus and urged him to tell him all the details, bringing him up to date prior to where the letter began. His face did not display any anger, nor did he become antagonistic, but instead showed relief.

"As you no doubt concluded, it is I that Paul is speaking of in this letter. I have been his companion and studied at his feet for quite some time now. He was like a father to me. I would give my life for him. He taught me so much and provided for me in a lot of ways. I also want to ask your forgiveness for the way that I treated you so many years ago and beg of you to let me make it up to you."

"So you are the runaway slave from so many years ago? We looked for you everywhere and just did not understand how you could have taken flight so quickly. I prayed for your safety because I just knew that something terrible had happened to you since we scoured the area and could not find you. I am only relieved to know that you are safe. I understand your parents were very distraught, and it was difficult for them to concentrate on their work."

"I am indeed Onesimus. Please tell me how I can make up for all the agony I have caused. I am not the same person I was then, being a youth and wanting to explore. I was determined to be free. I used to see all the people come and go and wanted desperately to be one of them. Then one evening, I got brave enough to make the move and do something about it. I presume that you know that I also took money from you and I am so sorry that I did that. It was just lying there out on the cart in the open and was such a temptation, knowing that I would not be able to survive if I did not have some kind of financial support. So I am guilty of this offense, too. That is what I have hated all these years — the fact that I actually stole from you. The sin that I committed tore me apart. I have asked the Lord to forgive me many times. Paul and I prayed over the entire situation often because that was my thorn in the flesh." Onesimus needed to get so much cleared up.

"I have taken this beautiful letter from Paul under advisement. I am not planning on punishing you in any way, please feel confident in that. I have been advised by Paul not to receive you as a pagan master, but as a Christian receives a brother. However, I am just wondering how you will be received by all the other servants who I have working here. I will call a meeting with all my officers and insist that they understand. I cannot possibly have you resume the role that you left so many years ago, Onesimus. After all, if you were Paul's right-hand man, how can I expect any less from you now even with me?" Philemon was trying to absorb this news he had just received.

"Paul has been praying that you would understand and I am confident that his prayers have touched you in a mighty way." Onesimus was careful how he approached his former master.

"You must know that actually I have mixed feelings as we speak. I am very relieved that you are safe, of course, but on the other hand, memories of when you left still linger in my mind. However, time does have a way of healing all wounds and I, as well, have prayed for God's intervention if this encounter ever occurred." Philemon was reflecting on time lost in lamenting over Onesimus.

"You do not know how very sorry I am for all the grief I must have cost you. Paul has assured me that God has had a purpose in it all." Onesimus was feeling very awkward.

"Tell me Onesimus, how long has Paul known?" Philemon trusted Paul's handling of the situation, but for his own peace of mind, he had to get that much resolved.

"I assure you, not very long at all. I cannot say for sure. But the part of my stealing from you is very new information to him," Onesimus was quick to explain.

"Have you seen your family yet? You may not realize that your father is not in good health, so you must go seek them out immediately. Your mother is still very vital in the kitchen, but your father does little work for me anymore; however, I continue to provide a place for him here. I will also have a comfortable room prepared for you and Tychicus to stay." Philemon assured the two of them.

"I am very delighted that you have traveled with Onesimus, Tychicus and I want to hear more regarding the trips you have taken for and with Paul. You have traveled to areas that he has not been able to, I am well aware. The church elders will be very excited in meeting with you both and hear firsthand how Paul is doing." Philemon was unable to think through what he must do with Onesimus at that moment.

"You are still smelling up the place with your fresh baked bread, I see." Onesimus said as he came behind his mother with a big hug around her waist. He could not wait to find his mother and see her excitement in knowing that her one and only son was home and safe.

"Onesimus, is that you? Yes, yes, I would recognize that voice anywhere. Come here and let me look at you. I have waited for a long time to be able to embrace you. Are you all right? Please tell me everything has happened to you. I have been very anxious about you. My, how you have grown." Leithia was sobbing very hard, but could not believe her eyes. She was so ecstatic.

Leithia took time out from her baking to sit and talk with Onesimus. She had never heard of Paul or any of his companions but realized he must be very special. She was not well-versed on his new God or anything pertaining to the Holy Spirit that had become her son's whole life. "Mother, it is so good to see you. You do not know how much I have missed you and I have thought of you often. I will tell you all about where I have been and what I have done. I will let you know everything that has happened to me since I left here. It will take some time, but I am sure that Philemon will allow us that. Let me help you serve the dinner and we will then have time to talk." Onesimus put his hand on his Mother's cheek to wipe away her tears of happiness.

After some time spent in getting caught up, she realized she needed to finish the duties she had begun on her own or else she would find herself in trouble. They agreed to meet together again after the evening meal, which would give him an opportunity to seek his father out and reassure him of his safety.

There was a big feast in the evening with the elders of the church joining Tychicus and Onesimus at Philemon's home. They were brought up to date on Epaphras and how he had been helping Paul out so much since his arrival at Paul's house while under arrest. There were many stories told, and Tychicus was delighted in knowing that the church there was growing in numbers as well as in the faith. Everyone was actually delighted to have Onesimus be a part of their group. It was refreshing to know how his past had intersected with Paul and how Philemon had received him so lovingly.

Onesimus shared with them that Paul's prison quarters were like an oasis in the desert because it refreshed the hearts of God's people. "One of the thoughts that Paul left me with is; 'as children of light our actions should reflect our faith and shine brightly to others. We should never be afraid to show our faith no matter where we are or who we are with. After all, we are beacons of God's love shining out into a dark world that is searching for love in all the wrong places – a world that is full of people without love, hope and faith'. I tell you that Paul is an ambassador in chains."

"I would like to have time this evening to meet with the church leaders in private now that we have finished our meal together. So, Onesimus and Tychicus, if you would please excuse us, we have matters we need to discuss." Philemon knew what he had to say to the elders had to be done in private.

"Thank you for coming out this evening and sharing with me decisions that need to be made as a result of information that has been brought to my attention through the letter that was carried by Tychicus and dictated by Paul. As you are aware this was the young man who abandoned me, and after many trials and hardships, found his way to Paul, and was led to the Lord. I am sure you can see in him something very special that can only come through a relationship with the Lord. You also should be aware that I could not possibly retain the services he had under his previous circumstances with me. That would certainly be a waste of the abilities that have been given to him. Paul asked a favor of me and you very well know that no man asks fewer favors than Paul. Onesimus took the wrong turn and Paul helped him find the way back." Philemon took into account the expressions and body language of the men he was addressing to see if they were thinking along the same lines.

"You may recall how we have spoken of having someone work with the slaves on our property to teach them the Gospel. We have been putting this off because we have not been able to find the right person. Do you not agree that Onesimus could be the one for whom we have been searching? He would be the perfect one to teach and witness to them. In doing so, it would not be offensive to them that I am not taking harsh means of retaliation."

"When word gets out, all eyes are going to be on you, Philemon, as to how you are going to handle a runaway slave and also, if you allow it this once, just think how it could be an example to others to do the same. Think about the other owners and the position you will put them in, not counting the attitude of your own slaves when you accept someone back with no consequences." Credo felt he had to be objective.

The others around the table nodded their heads in agreement. Taking all these thoughts into consideration and after sharing their opinions, looking at the situation from all angles and re-reading Paul's letter, it was decided that Philemon would make the arrangements with Onesimus first thing in the morning.

Having brought his mother and father up to date on everything that had happened in the last few years, their emotions were a combination of joy, ecstasy, gratitude and pride. They wanted to know all about Paul; what a special person he must be. They wanted to go kiss the feet of Philemon because they had always feared for Onesimus's safety if he had ever been found. Onesimus assured them of Philemon's love for the Lord and it was because of God's grace that he had been accepted back in a loving manner.

Onesimus realized he needed to give his mother and father some alone time because he wanted them to especially know his Lord and have the love of the Lord Jesus Christ. After having heard 'his story', they could contemplate this freedom they, too, could feel in their lives. He wanted them to have what he had.

"You will be elevated here. In fact I have just the right position for you." Philemon was explaining all the details to

Onesimus and how it had the seal of approval from all the other church leaders.

"You are too kind. I did not expect to come back here and fall so overwhelmingly under your graces. I had every intention to take up where I left off. I am sure you have someone working the stables, and caring for the livestock, but there are surely other things I could do to help out." Onesimus wanted to be sure Philemon knew he was not asking for favors.

"Please let me explain to you what I have in mind. If you do not think it will work out, feel free to let me know." Philemon assured Onesimus there was indeed a plan.

"I am listening and will do whatever you ask." Onesimus knew he owed his master that much.

"The thought has come to me that you could be a consultant for the other slaves. I understand that you have become well versed in the Word of the Lord. We had always tried our best to make it so that our servants have a good life here. Now we will have a new plan set up. I also want them to draw closer to Jesus Christ. That has been my passion for quite some time, but I was not sure how to orchestrate it until now. You could be the one to see that it happens. As long as they do the work expected of them, they will be able to come to you for teaching. The other servants will only need to know that you have been away taking a special training. Now that your training is complete, you are ready to serve me again, only this time in the capacity of teacher and the other servants will be your students. I want them to know Jesus. I mean really know Him. Are you willing to do that for me?" Philemon knew he did not have to ask. He could tell right away the excitement in Onesimus's face.

"I have been taught to read. I read God's word every day and it has blessed me so much that I do not know how I could have survived without it. Sometimes I read to Paul when he was too tired to do so, which was most of the time because he had a really hard time seeing the words. Then we would discuss and he would explain what I had read. Yes, yes I would love this position." Onesimus was now feeling very excited and could not wait to let Tychicus know what his new position would be.

"Then, that is settled. I know what we need to have you do. It is very customary to allow slaves to attend worship with their Christian masters. This is something that I have not adopted here so much because I am not aware of any believers who serve me. First of all I will have Bastien gather all the men together and explain to them what will take place. You will be introduced as their teacher and they are to respect your leadership. They will know the time and place to meet after they have finished with their duties. You will then read to them from God's Word, and I understand you will be able to explain to them the law and prophets. This should prove to be very beneficial for them and hopefully, they will realize that they are a part of God's kingdom. How do you think that plan will work, Onesimus?" Philemon thought it a very good idea, but was anxious to hear how Onesimus felt about its coming to fruition. He could have put it in the form of an order, but instead wanted to show some kindness to his new brother in the Lord.

"Can you not tell that I am very excited about the suggestion? I think this is an excellent idea, and I hope that it will catch on so that more households will adopt the idea. With your approval, I am ready and anxious to get started with this as soon as possible." Onesimus knew about God's sovereignty and this was a confirmation of that fact.

The situation had been molded and shaped into a teamwork endeavor.

No longer was it a master/slave relationship, but more like a partnership.

After the letter to the church of Colossae had been delivered, Tychicus was glad to have an opportunity to speak with Philemon alone, "That was very noble in the way you handled the situation with Onesimus. I realize that having the advice of Paul was a huge contribution, but the decision on how you regarded Onesimus was truly your call."

"As Paul stated, I am not obligated to accept Onesimus as a brother, but since he has become a brother to Paul and he and I are brothers, then Onesimus is also a brother of mine. How do you treat a brother except with respect and dignity? That is the least I can do. I owe Paul my own life. What kind of repayment would it be to turn my back on Onesimus?" Philemon was confident in his feelings.

"I must ask you one thing on behalf of Paul." Tychicus remembered Paul's instructions.

"Anything. I will do anything for Paul, you know that." Philemon was curious to know what Tychicus was going to ask.

"This letter needs to be circulated among the church people here. Will that be a problem with you to allow the church fellowship to read it? That was Paul's request." Tychicus needed to make sure that the appeal came from Paul and not himself.

"It would be very acceptable to me. There is nothing in it to hide. I believe that would be very encouraging to the people at the church here just to hear messages directly from Paul himself." Philemon thought that was an easy task to carry out. "I think the church here needs to be aware of Paul's thoughts. They need to specifically be aware about the part of 'welcoming him as you would me' for there is not a man here who would not be on the welcoming committee for Paul's visit."

"Paul told me what a righteous man you are and now I see for myself what he was talking about," Tychicus added.

"We each will anticipate the visit that he plans on making here. I only hope and pray it will happen soon, and we will definitely have a room ready for Paul. Always." Philemon said with delight.

Chapter 19

"Onesimus, I am very proud of what you have accomplished here with all my servants. Ever since you began working with them and teaching them the Gospel, they have had a different attitude as they work. I have noticed they have bonded more toward each other. It is like they have a reason to live. Their life, because of learning of the Lord, is more vital to them." Philemon enjoyed complimenting and encouraging Onesimus every chance he got.

"I do appreciate your confirmation in what I am trying to accomplish with them. I do take this position very seriously." Onesimus was actually enjoying seeing the growth of the servants.

"If there is anything I can personally do for you, please do not hesitate to let me know. You have been working so hard in getting this program organized and implementing its process, you may even like to take some time off." As Philemon spoke he noticed how Onesimus took pleasure in that suggestion.

"As a matter of fact, I do have someplace I would love to go. I would not be gone long at all, but there is someone I met along the way who is now living in Miletus and I would love more than anything to go there for a visit." Onesimus could not believe how happy he was at the prospect of being able to see Tisha again.

"Yes, I think that can be arranged. How much time would you need to be away that would give you time to have a very nice visit with him?" Philemon noticed Onesimus's look of sheepishness at that comment.

"Oh, I think about a week will be a perfect length of time; however, I must confess to you that it is a 'her' that I would like to go see." Onesimus was fearful that it might change things now that he had revealed this fact.

"Oh, I see. May we go over here under the shade of the fig tree, sit awhile and you can fill me in on as much as you feel you can." Philemon's curiosity was certainly aroused by now.

A considerable amount of time had gone by and Philemon completely encouraged Onesimus to pursue this relationship. "The fact that she waited for you for such a long time is evidence in itself that she has strong feelings for you."

"I thought about that as well. Tisha will be thrilled to see me again, since we have been separated for a very long time. If it is all right with you, I will explain to the workers that I will be gone for a week and we will resume our lessons after that.

Am I hearing that it will be all right for me to go to Miletus the day after tomorrow?" Onesimus wanted to be certain he had Philemon's interests in place first and foremost.

"That is a wonderful plan. I would love to meet this Tisha and her son Julian, I believe. So if this relationship grows, and you feel led to do so, please invite them here." Philemon thought of Onesimus as a part of his family now.

Onesimus went out with joy as he traveled to Miletus thinking how much differently the trip was now than it had been when he had left before. He was now a free man with the weight of the world having been lifted from his shoulders. He had the love and grace of the Lord living within him and he was focusing on a life with Tisha.

The trip to Miletus went much faster than before, especially since he was able to travel on the main roads and not have to be in fear of capture.

"Will she feel the same as I do? Will she accept me after I really share with her all of my past life? I feel so close to Tisha that I must hold onto the thought that she has the same desires as I." Onesimus could not help the thoughts that were running through his mind as he walked along. He finally dismissed any negative feelings and concentrated on her sweet face and enjoyment he had with her.

Before he knew it, he was in Miletus and even though he was physically exhausted from pushing himself to get there, he began running down the dusty road that took him through the little town. He kept up his pace until he saw her house in the distance. He continued on with a gallop all the way to the little path that led to her front door.

He had not realized how thrilled he was to be able to share with her the fact that he had a life of his own and would be able to include her in it if she were willing. "I am finally here," he said to himself. "I cannot believe my heart is pounding so hard."

As he brought his arm up to knock on the door, it was opened by a beautiful and radiant face that said. "I knew you would come back".

Biblical Individuals Summarized

Apphia – The wife of Philemon and mother of Archippus who lived in the area of Colossae.

Archippus – son of Philemon and Apphia He is mentioned in Col 4;17 Phil 1:2

Aristachus – was from Thessalonica and accompanied Paul from Greece to Macedonia as well as many other travels. He shared Roman imprisonment wit Paul. Acts 27:2

Demas – A fellow-worker and companion of Paul while he was in Rome. Col 4:14, 2 Tim 4:10

Epaphras,–He was the **founder** of the church at Colossae and the catalyst for evangelism in the Lycus Valley. Paul probably led him to Christ, Col

1:7 The church at Colosse may have sent Epaphras to Rome to minister to Paul in jail and while there he was imprisoned as well.

John Mark – After having spurned him during Paul's first missionary travels, he recognized the value of Mark. He later wrote to Timothy, urging him to 'get Mark and bring him with you for he is useful to me for ministry" – 2 Tim 4:11.

Justus – His home adjoined the synagogue in Corinth. He received Paul when other Jews opposed him. He was always a comfort to Paul. Acts 18:7.

Onesimus – His name means 'useful' or 'profitable' and proved to be so in many ways. He was owned by Philemon, whom he ran away from but returned to him after coming to faith.

Paul – apostle for the Lord, imprisoned in Rome for speaking wholeheartedly for the Lord. Brought many to the Jesus while in chains.

Philemon- Was a wealthy businessman and land owner in the area of Colossae and owner of many slaves. He hosted groups of believers in his home.

Timothy – Met Paul during Paul's first missionary journey to Lystra. He was an ambassador for Paul and had authority to ensure the churches were doing things in a way that would be pleasing to Christ. He was considered as "Paul's own son" and never let him down. 2 Cor.1:1, Acts 16:1

Tychicus –Paul sent him to Ephesus to build up the church there. He was one of the last people mentioned by Paul before his death. 2 Tim 4:12. He was the person that carried Paul's prison letters to the Ephesians, Colossians, Philemon.